ABOUT

Tides and Other Works for Piano is a book of sheet music for the compositions featured on my solo piano album, *Tides* (New Focus Recordings, 2020). This book is intended for intermediate or advanced pianists who have a classical music background, a solid sense of jazz and modern harmony, and a strong internal rhythm.

I have been composing and recording music for large and small ensembles for almost 20 years. I realized in 2018 that certain compositions of mine became too dependent upon other musicians in order to be played fully. To free the music from these constraints, I decided instead to focus my writing on producing a body of work exclusively for the piano.

I strive to write music that is complex, yet enjoyable and comfortable to play. While writing these compositions, the word "pianistic" often came to mind: not only does the material "fit well" on the hand, but it also includes many "pianistic tricks," such as rhythmic/repetitive two-handed figures. As a pianist, this project has been extremely gratifying and challenging for me—and I am convinced that these pieces will also be inspiring for others to play.

NOTES

A few of the pieces have sections for optional improvisation:

In "Tortuga", there is a section right before letter E where the interpreter can improvise a solo on top of a written left hand, and gradually accelerate the tempo until reaching the tempo primo. From there, continue to the next section. If the pianist decides not to improvise, they can repeat the left-hand pattern four times until reaching the tempo primo, and continue to the next section.

In "Rio", there is a 6-bar chord progression and a suggested left hand in which the interpreter can decide whether to improvise a solo, or just play the repeat as written. and continue with the next section.

In "Playing", letter D has an optional 8-bar improvised fill that works as a transition from the fast section to the slow section. The interpreter can decide whether to improvise or to play the section as written.

As heard on the album, I improvised short introductions to "Tides" and "Eyelashes". The short preludes work well: as transitions between pieces, and as a breather to counterweight bigger chunks of written music. I encourage the interpreter to take a similar approach, and to feel free to improvise short preludes and interludes inside the pieces.

I hope you enjoy this book as much as I enjoyed writing these pieces.

Emilio Teubal,
New York, 2020

Published by Emilio Teubal (BMI)

Artwork and design by Alex Rearick
Music Engraving by Felipe Traine

emilioteubal.com

TIDES

Emilio Teubal

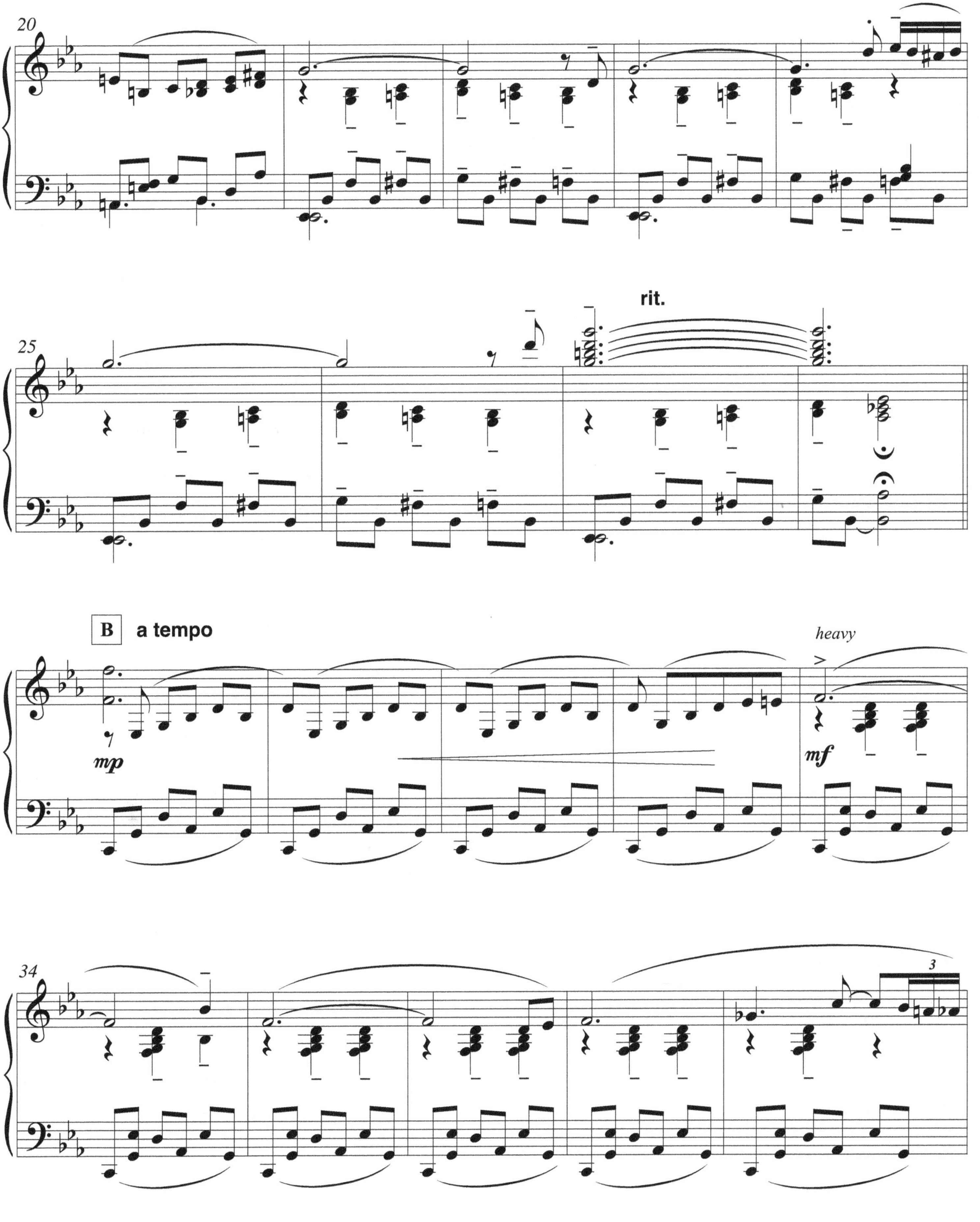
20
25
rit.
B
a tempo
heavy
mp
mf
34
3

Tides

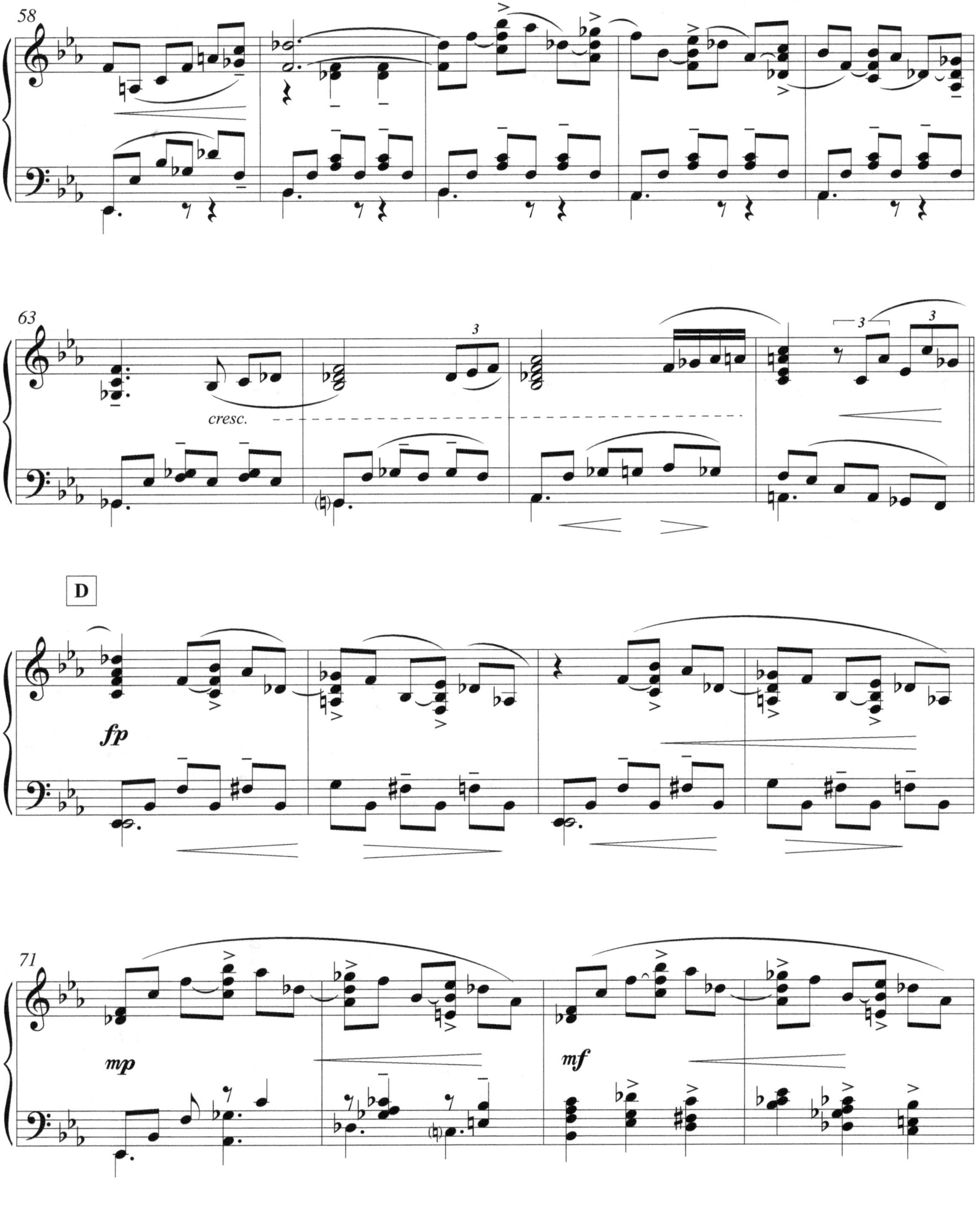
58
63
cresc.
D
fp
71
mp
mf

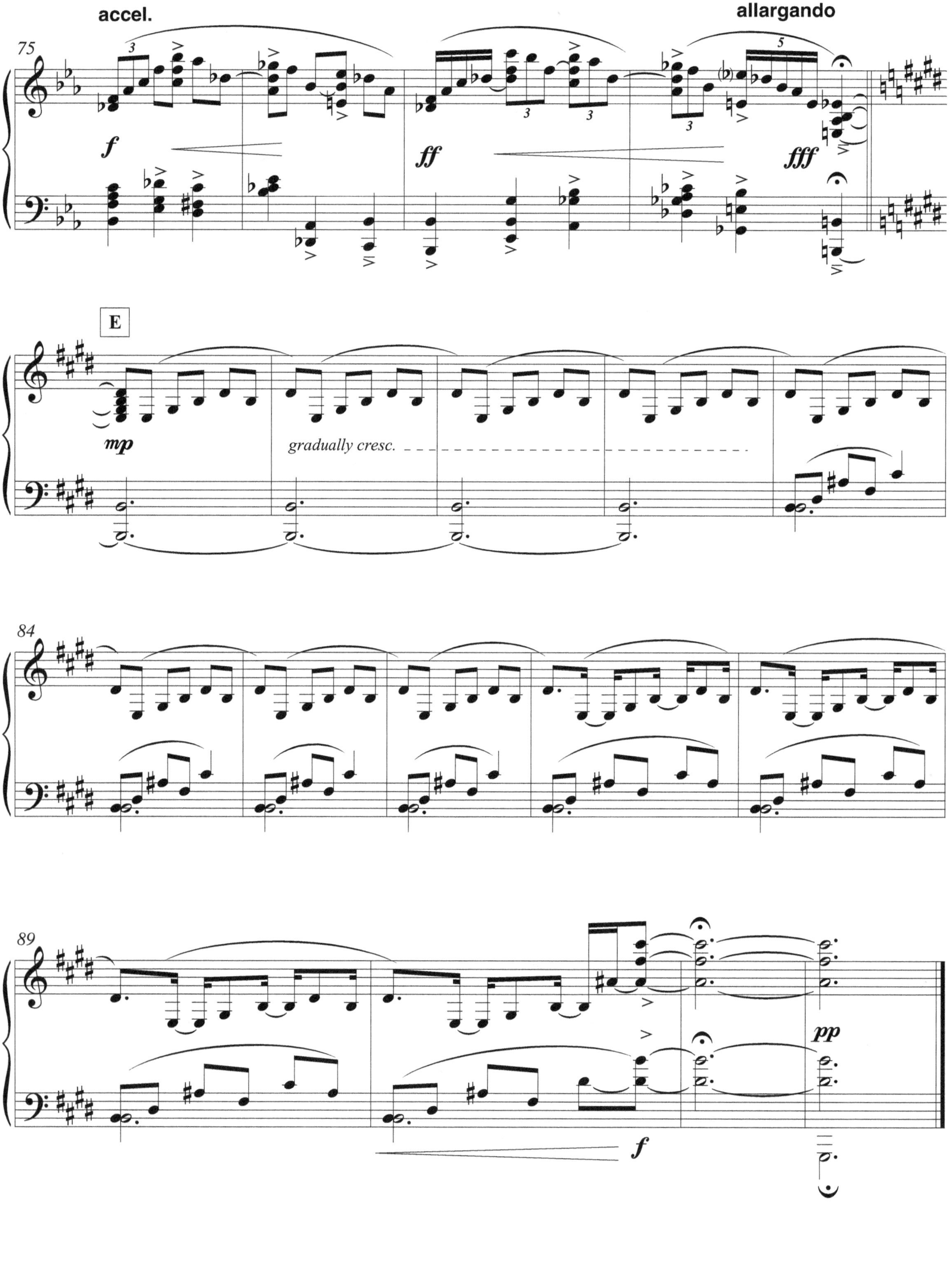
accel.
allargando
75
f
ff
fff
E
mp
gradually cresc.
84
89
f
pp

TORTUGA

to Julie Garber

Emilio Teubal

Tortuga

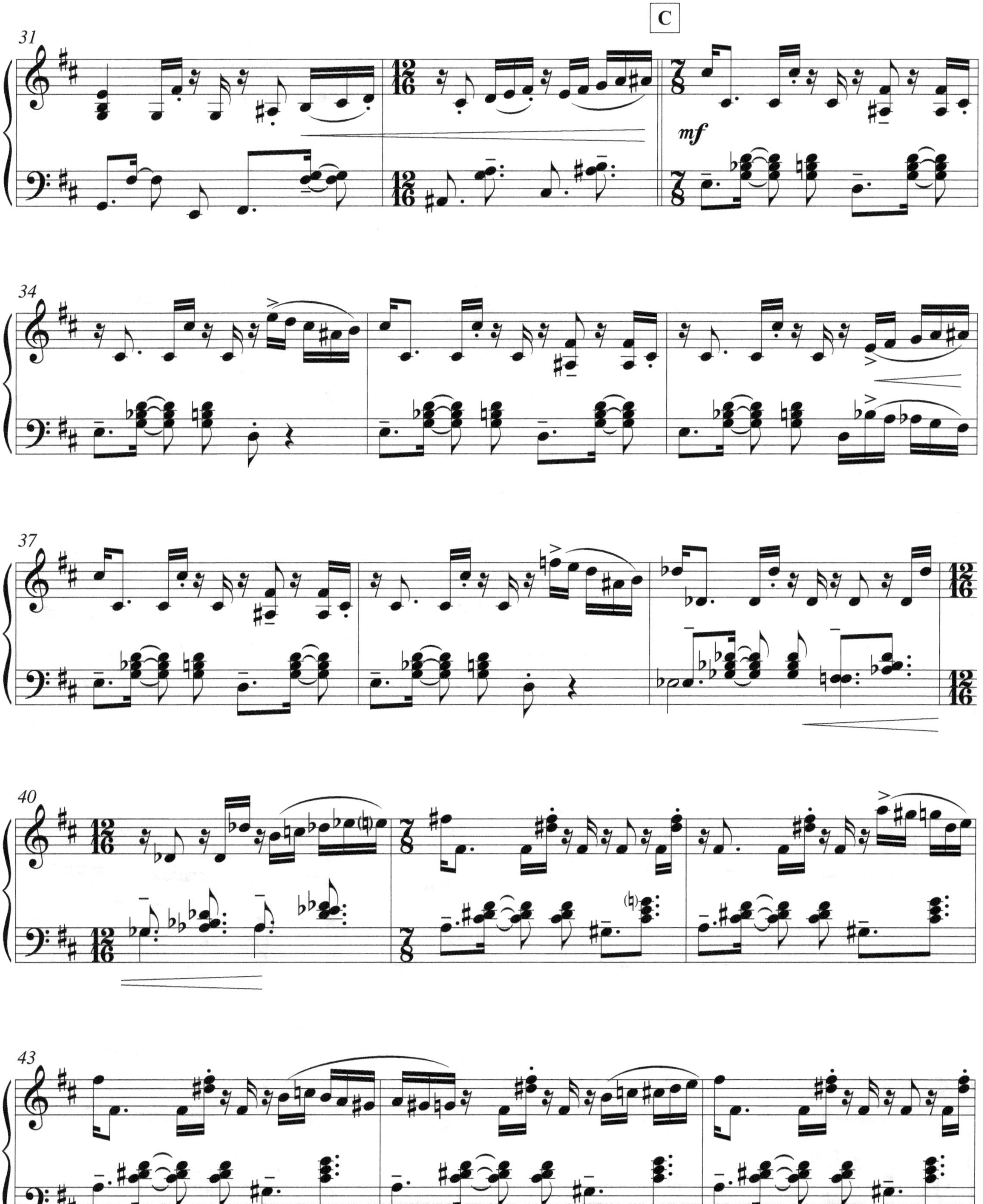
C
31
mf
34
37
40
43

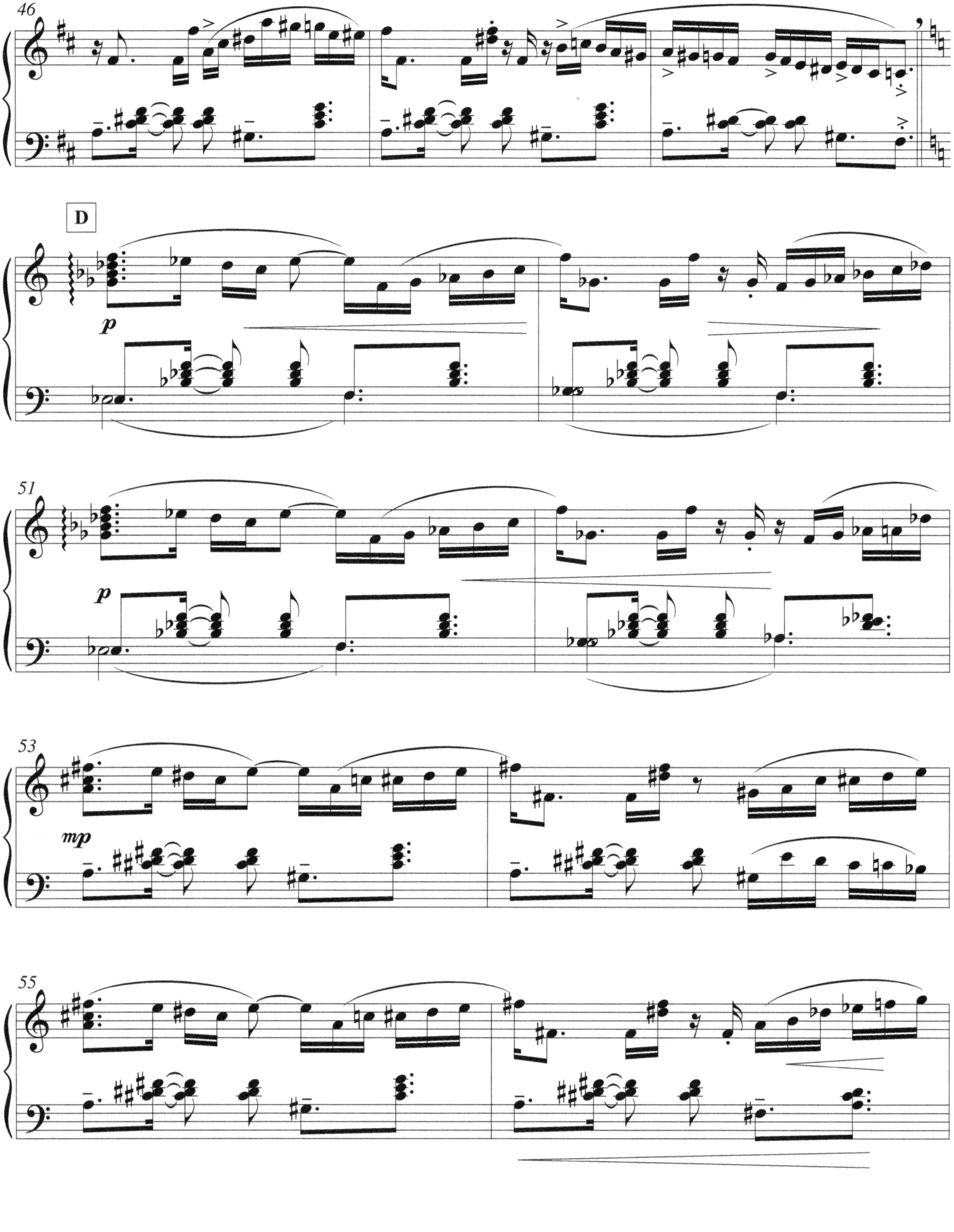
46
D
p
51
p
53
mp
55

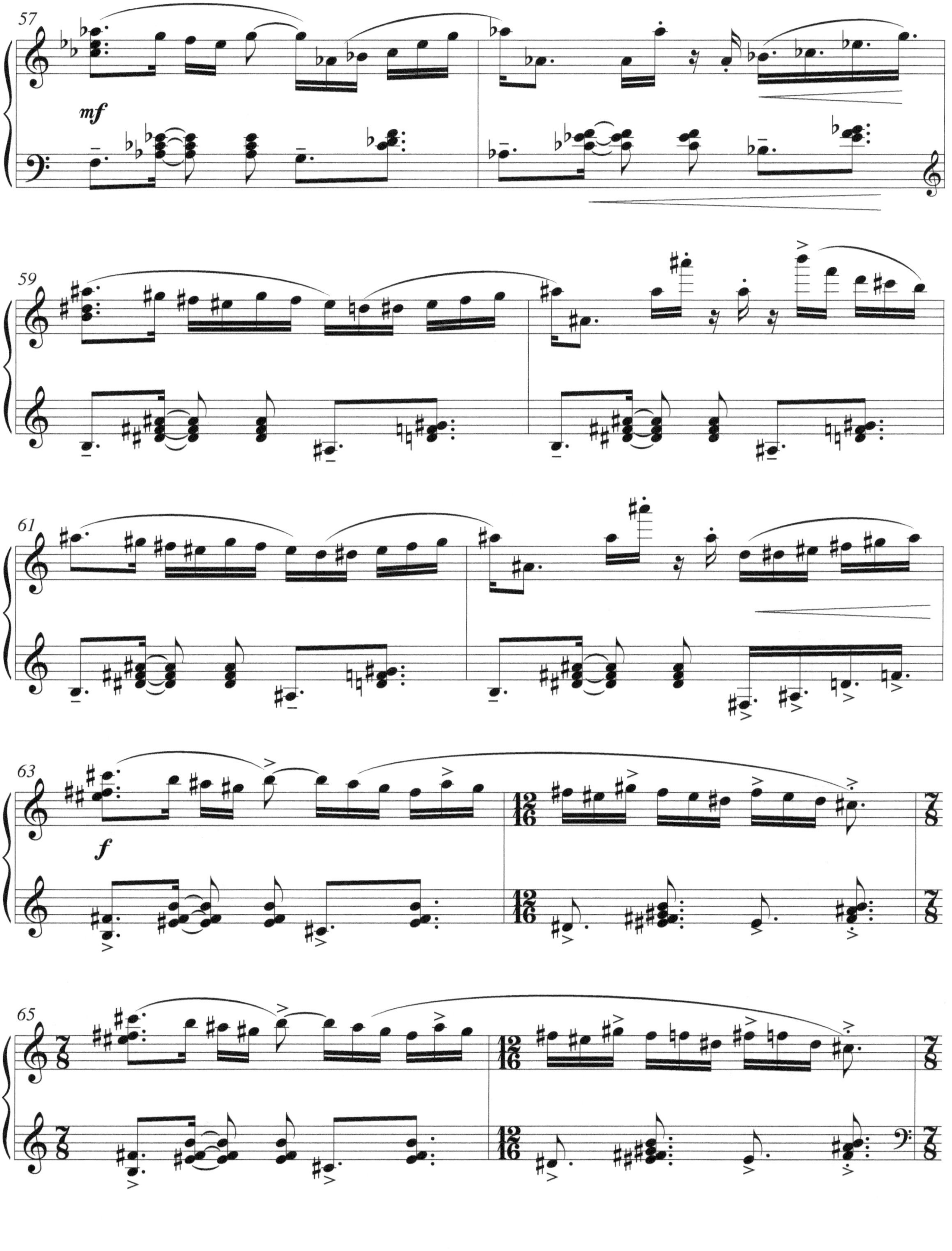
57
mf
59
61
63
f
65

Tortuga

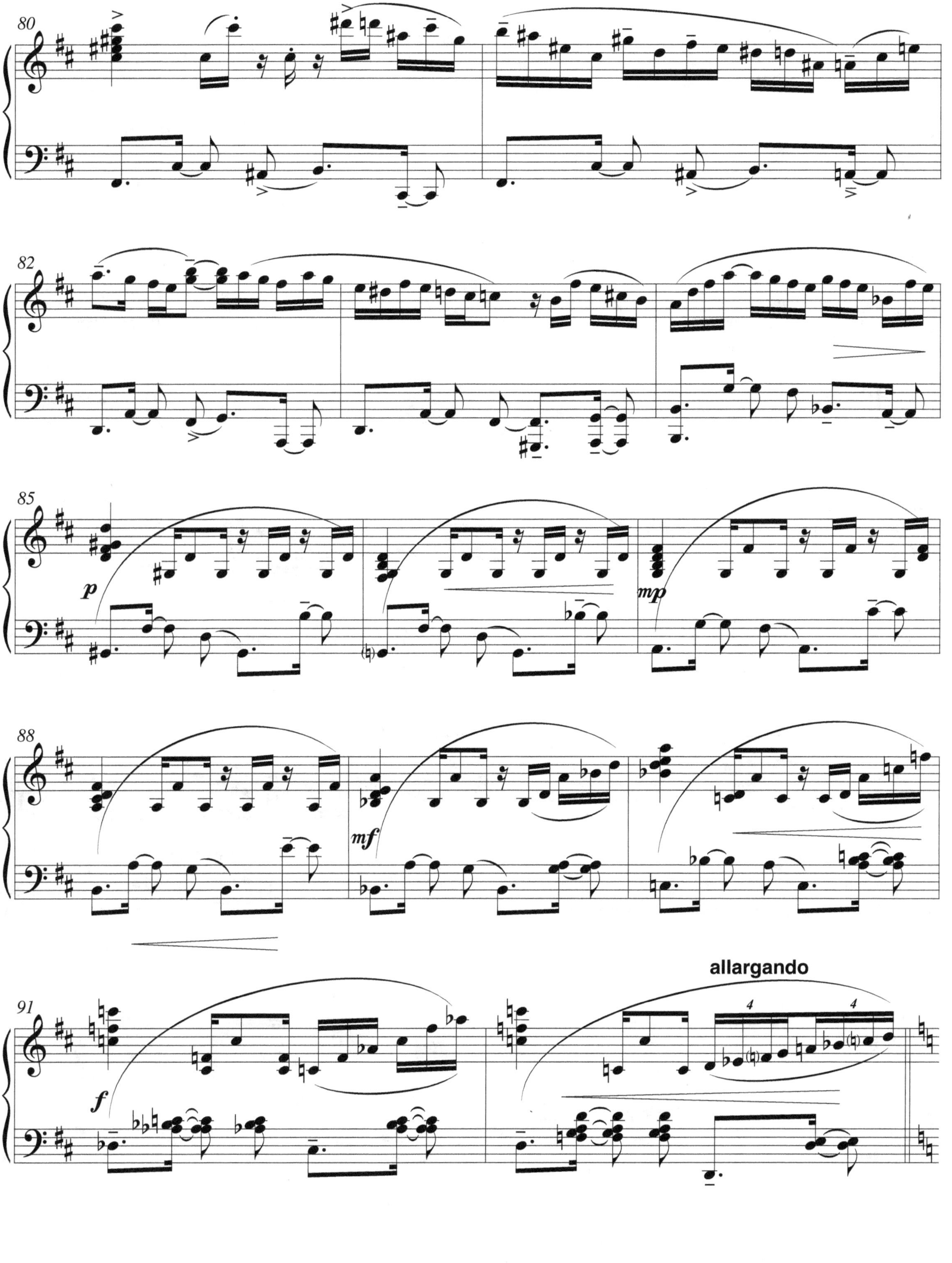
80
82
85
p
mp
88
mf
allargando
91
f

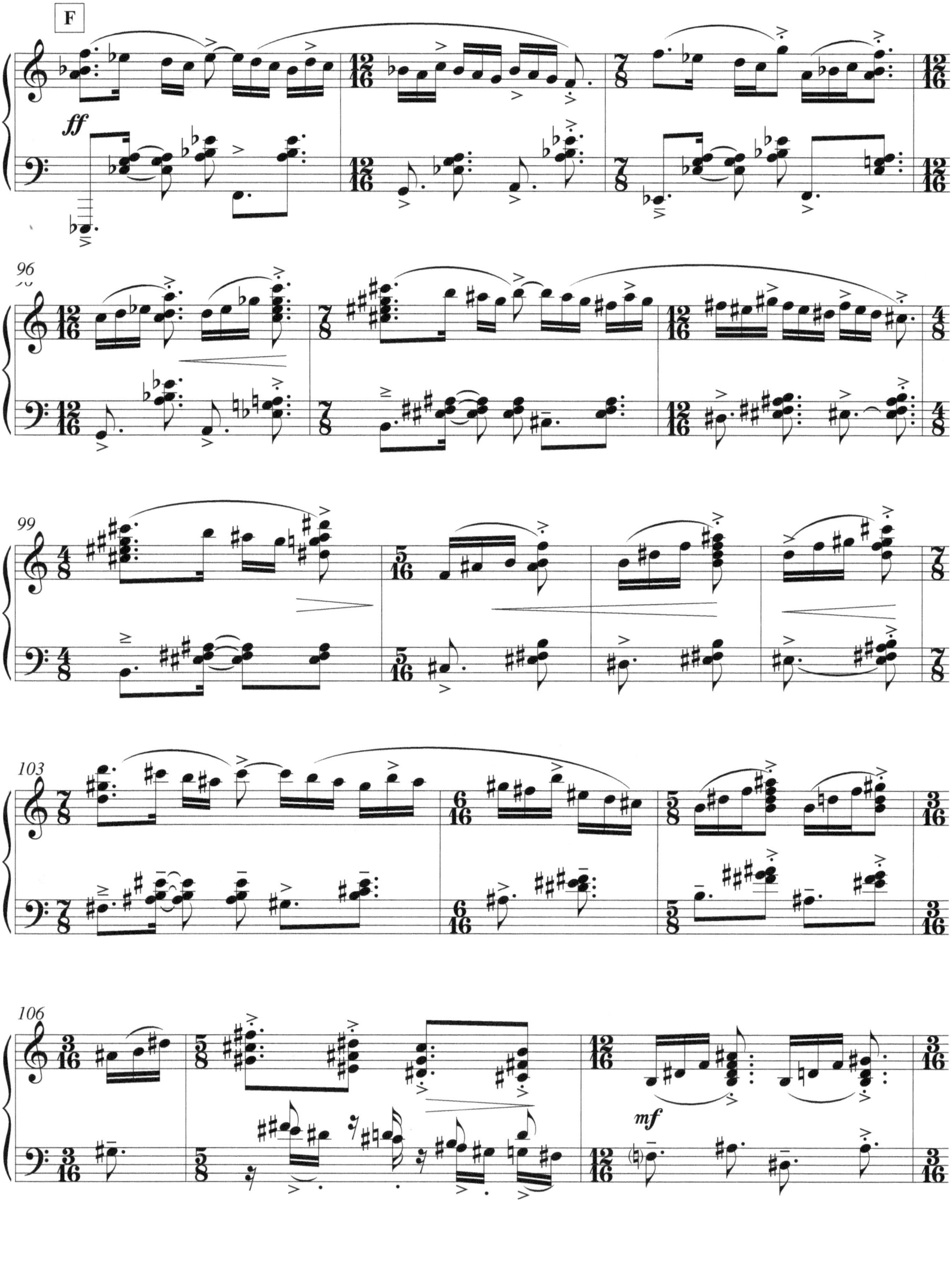
F
ff
96
99
103
106
mf

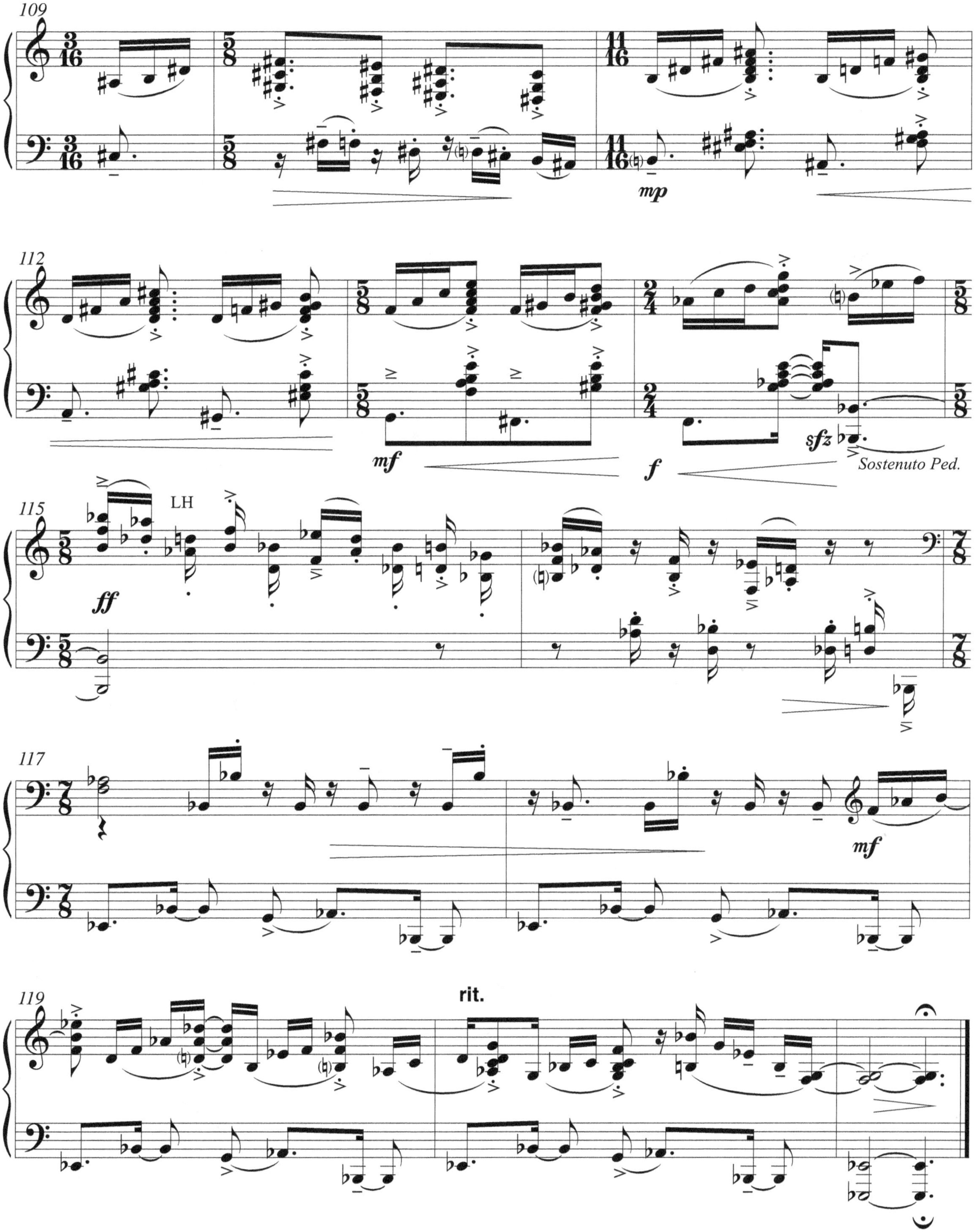
109
mp
112
mf
f
sfz
Sostenuto Ped.
115
LH
ff
117
mf
119
rit.

TIEMPO

to Miguel Teubal

Emilio Teubal

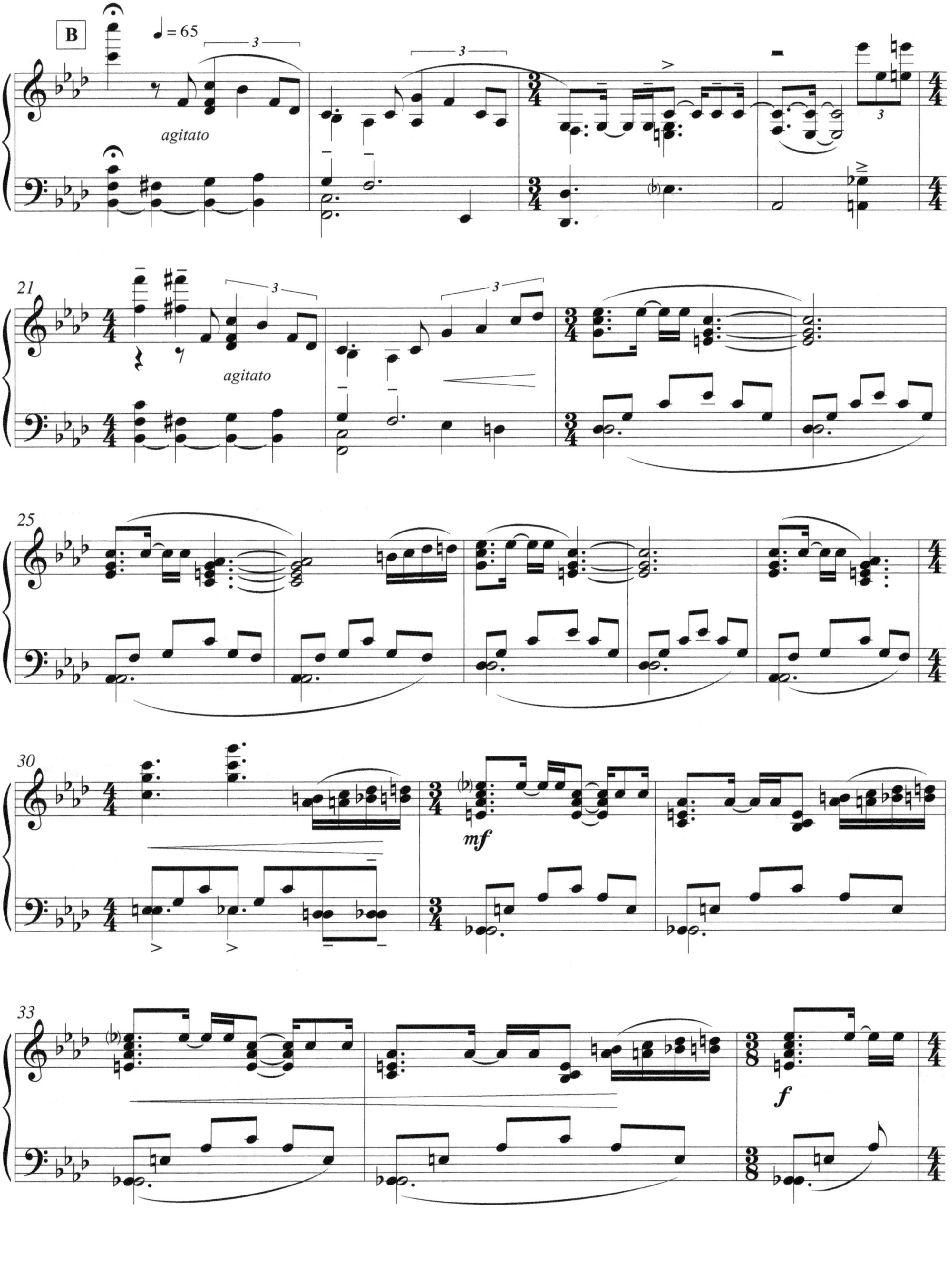
B
♩ = 65
agitato
21
agitato
25
30
mf
33
f

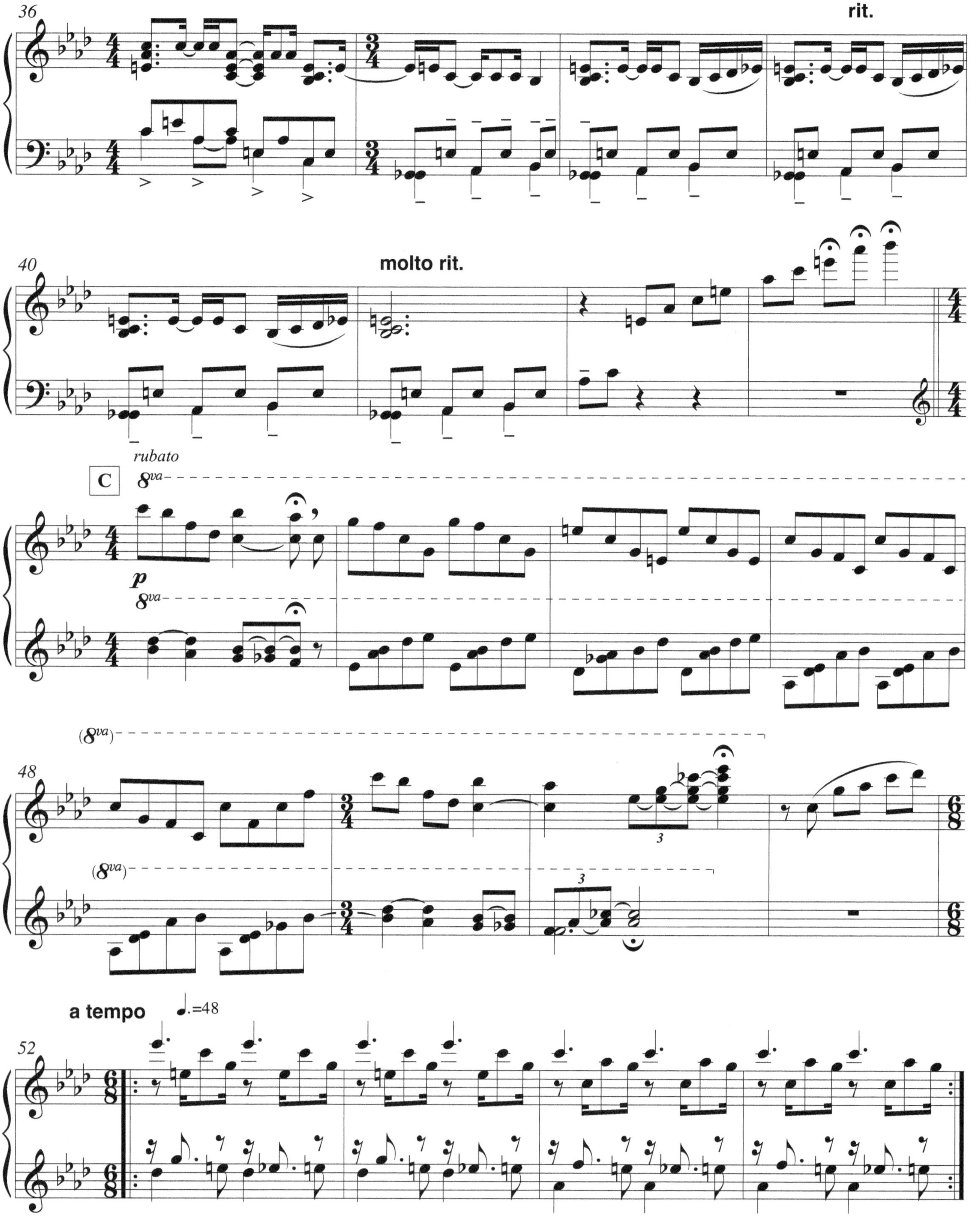
36
rit.
40
molto rit.
rubato
C
8va
p
8va
(8va)
48
3
(8va)
3
a tempo
♩.=48
52

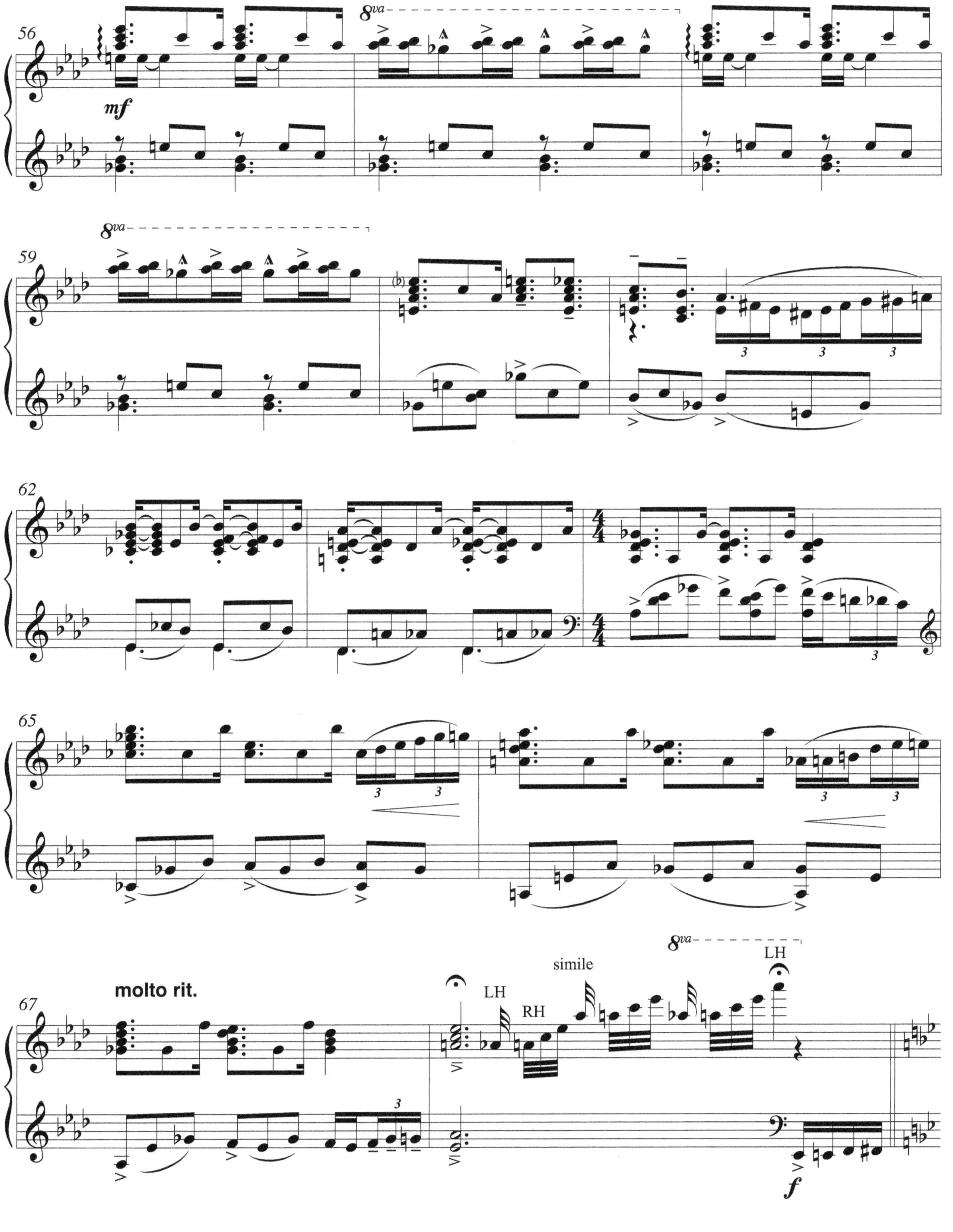
56
mf
8va
59
8va
62
4/4
65
67
molto rit.
LH
RH
simile
8va
LH
f

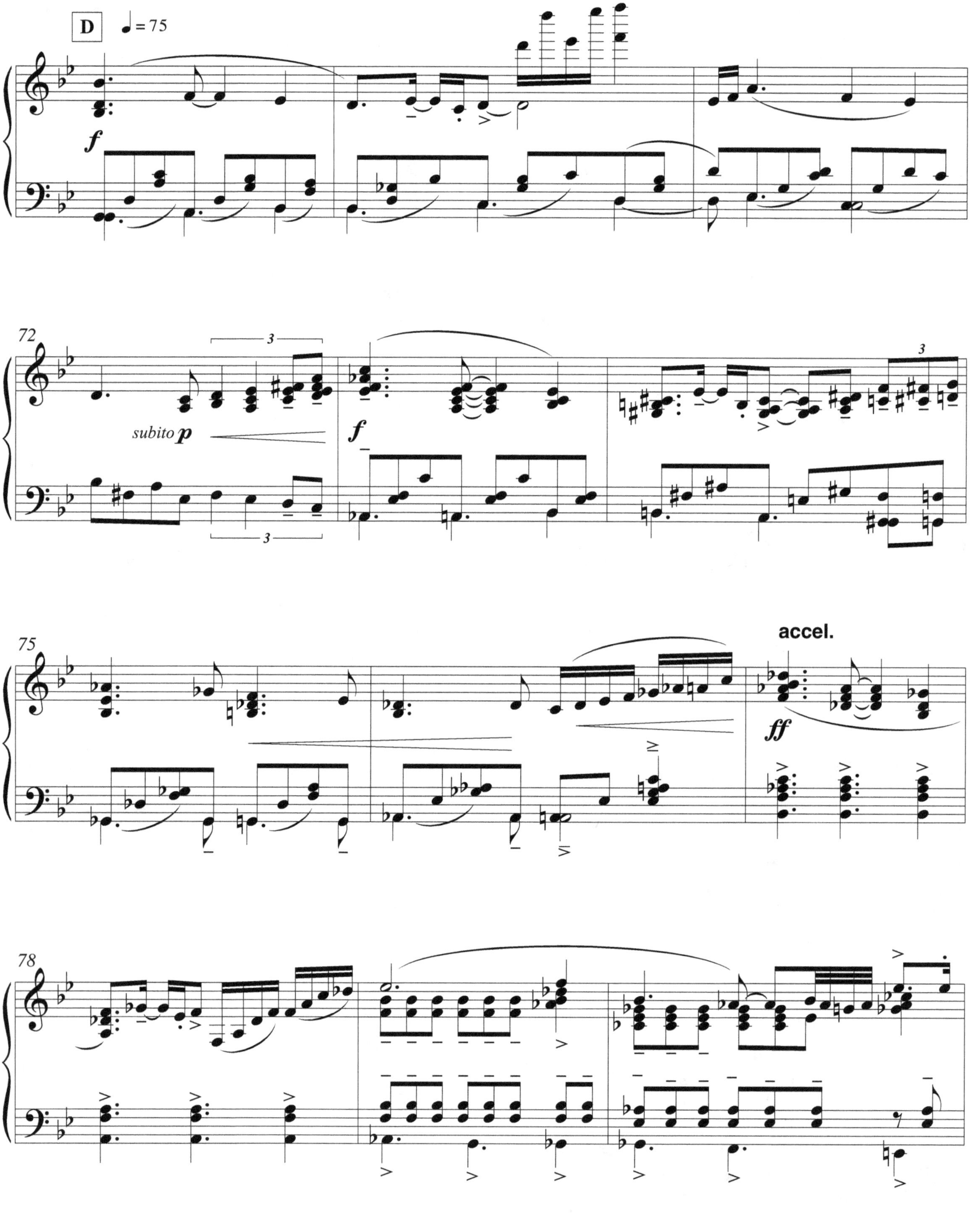
D
♩ = 75
f
72
3
subito p
f
3
75
accel.
ff
78

81
molto accel.
84
♩= 92
fff
87
90
mf
93
molto rit.
mp
rubato
8va
mf
ppp

RIO

Emilio Teubal

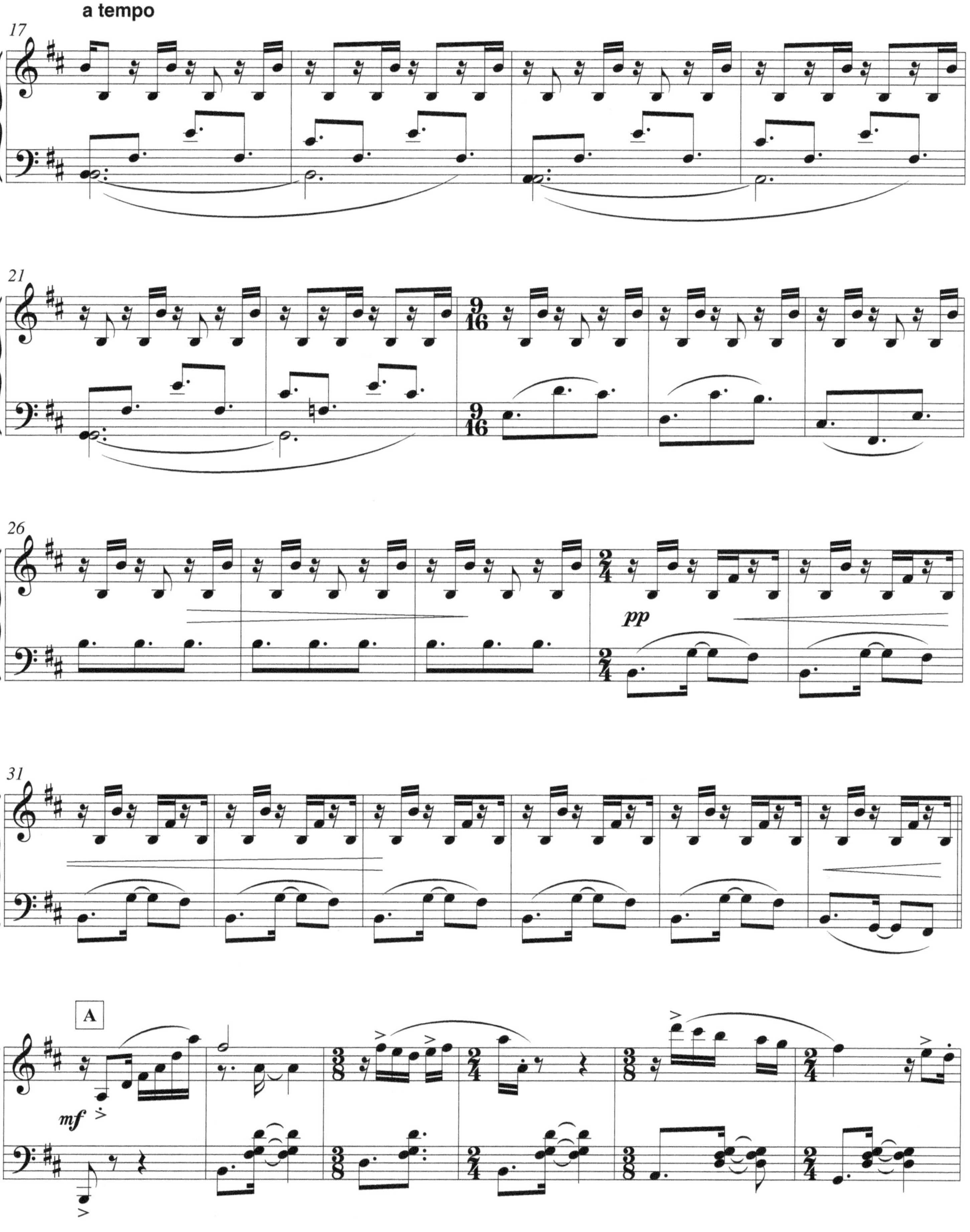
a tempo
17
21
26
pp
31
A
mf

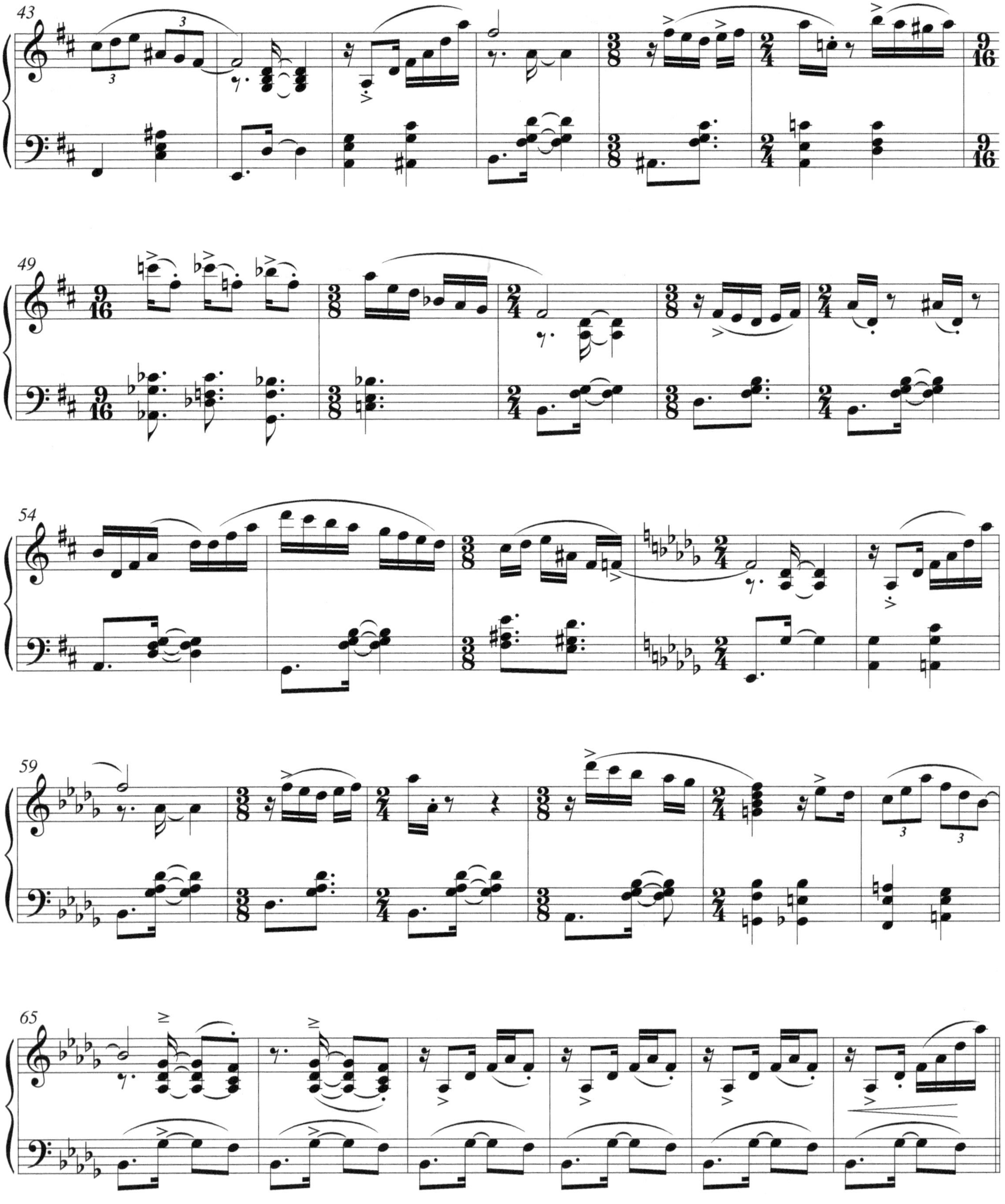

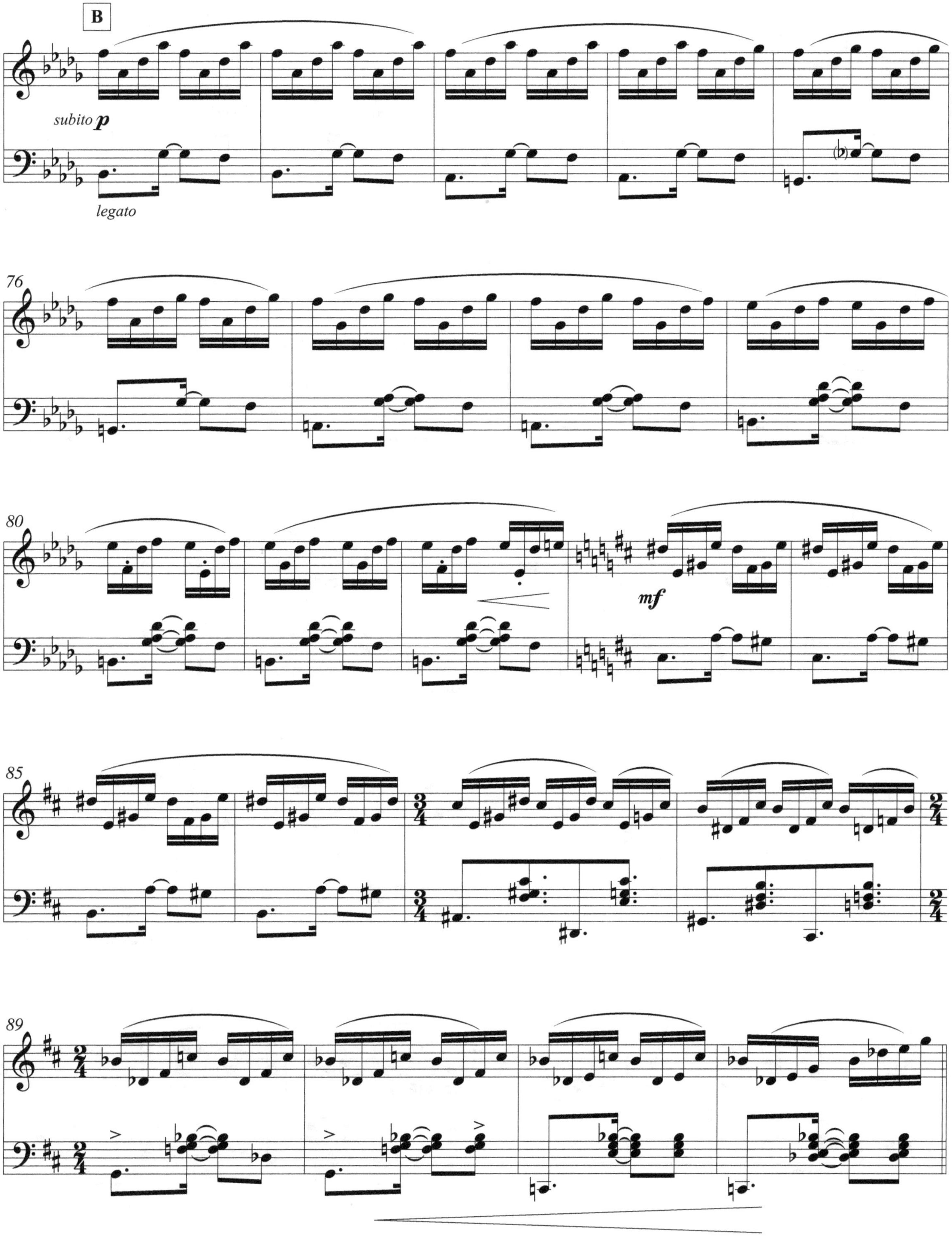
B
subito p
legato
76
80
mf
85
89

Rio

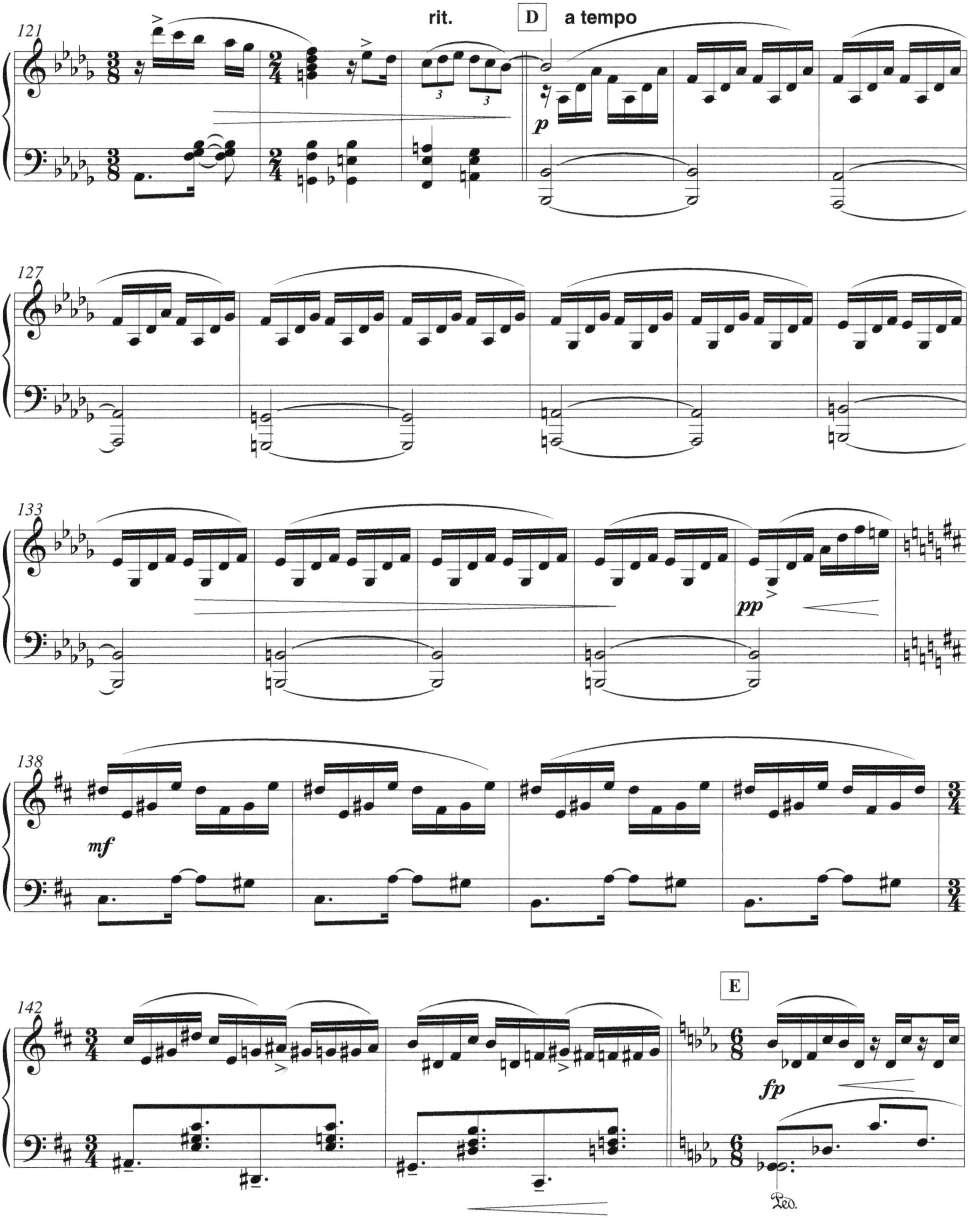
121
rit.
D
a tempo
p
127
133
pp
138
mf
142
E
fp
Ped.

Rio

Sostenuto Pedal

S.P

S.P

Rio

EYELASHES

A **Lento** 𝅗𝅥 = 40

Emilio Teubal

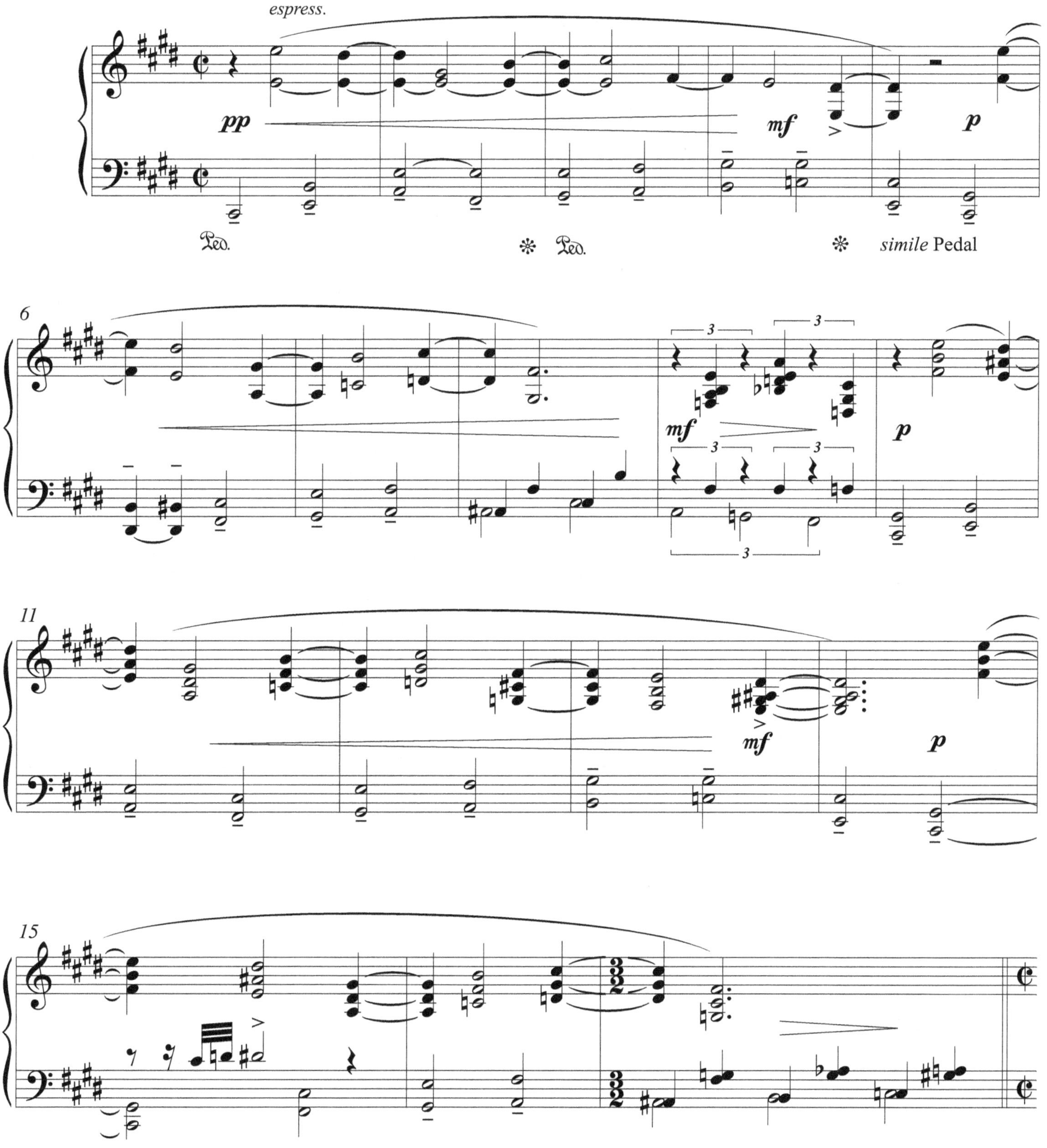

Eyelashes

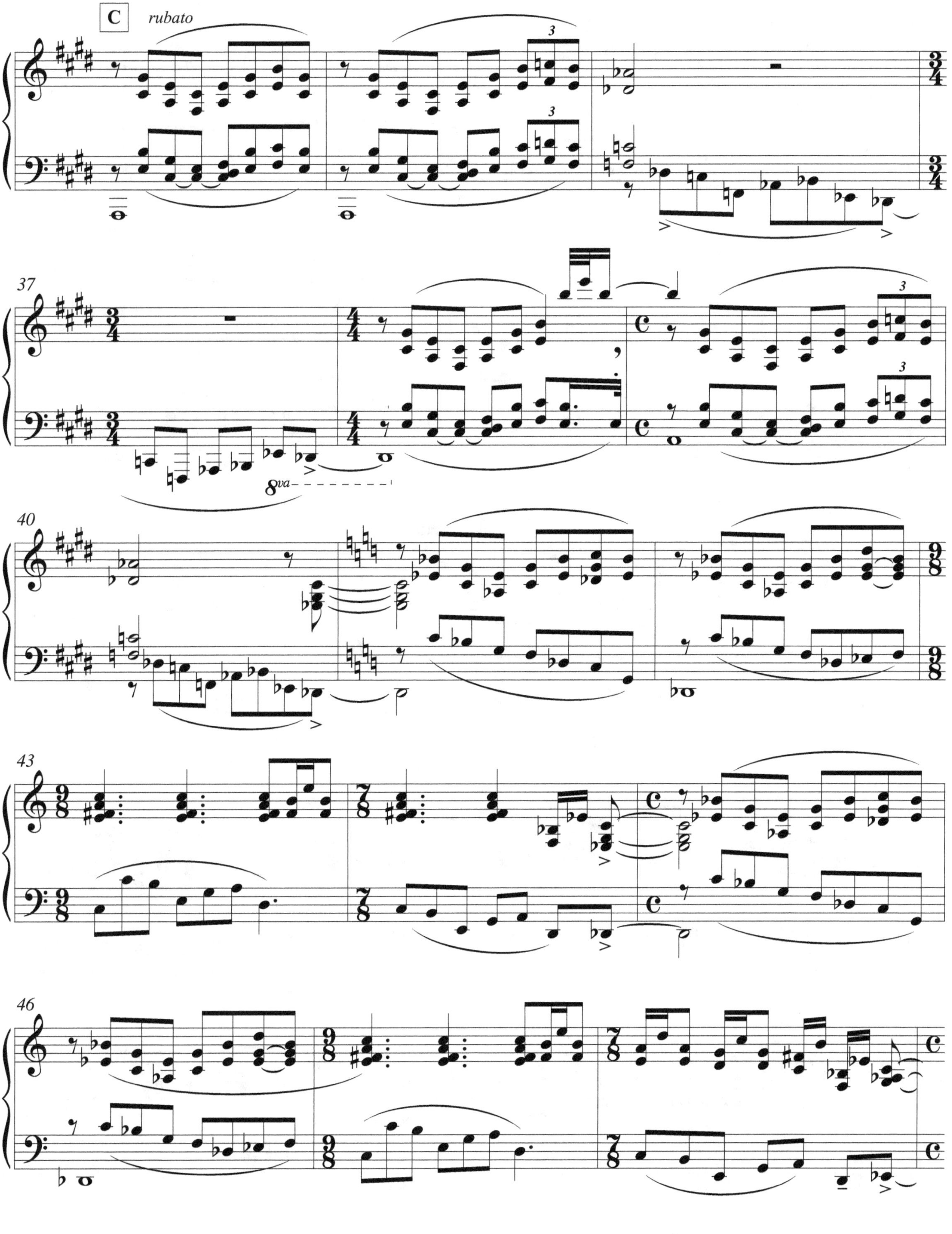
C
rubato
37
8va
40
43
46

Eyelashes

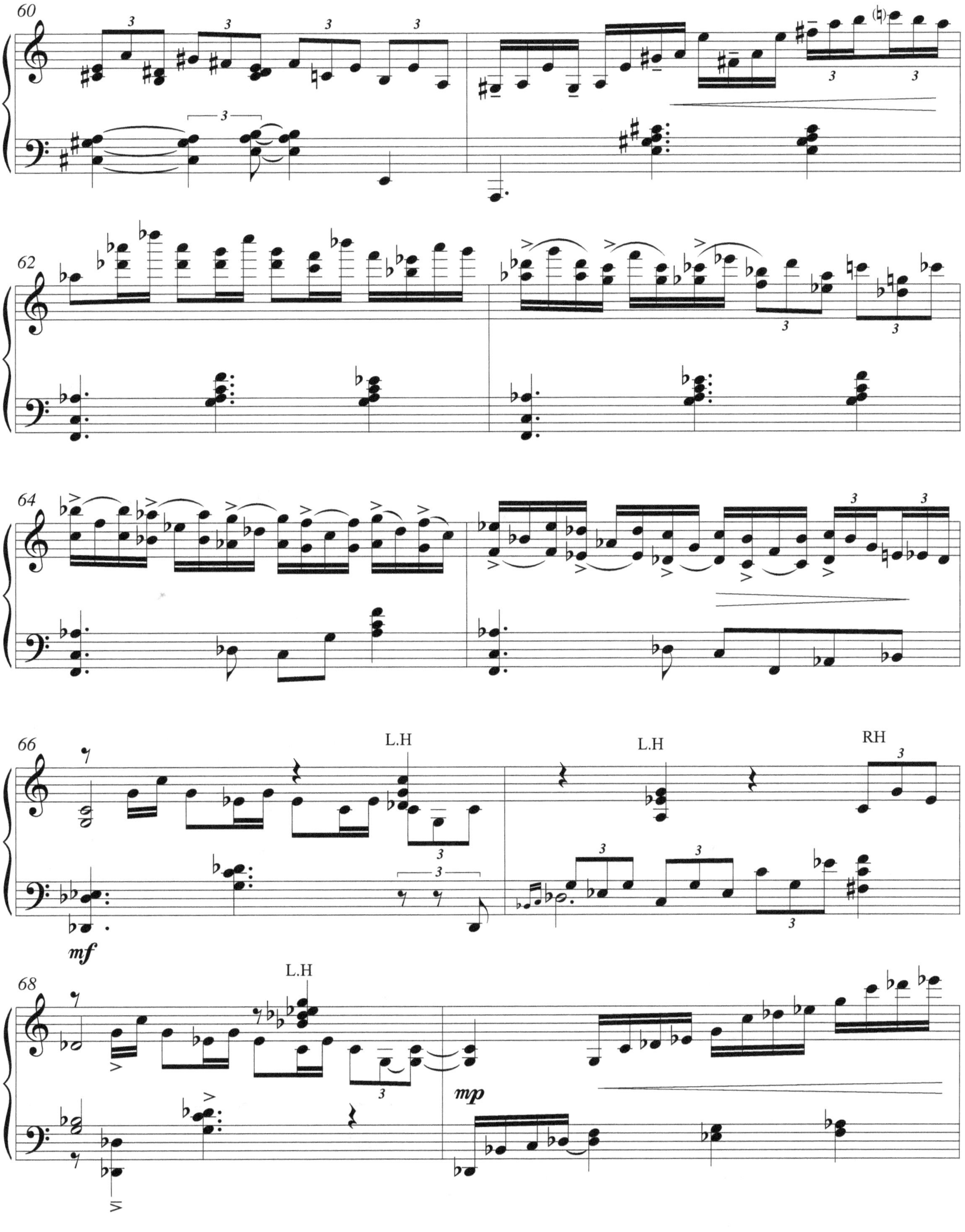
60
62
64
66
L.H
L.H
RH
mf
68
L.H
mp

Eyelashes

E
molto espress.
p
mf
82
84
molto espress.
mf
mp
mf
87
mp
mf
mp
90
mf
rit.
molto rit.

PLAYING

to Ema, Lidu and Tupac

Emilio Teubal

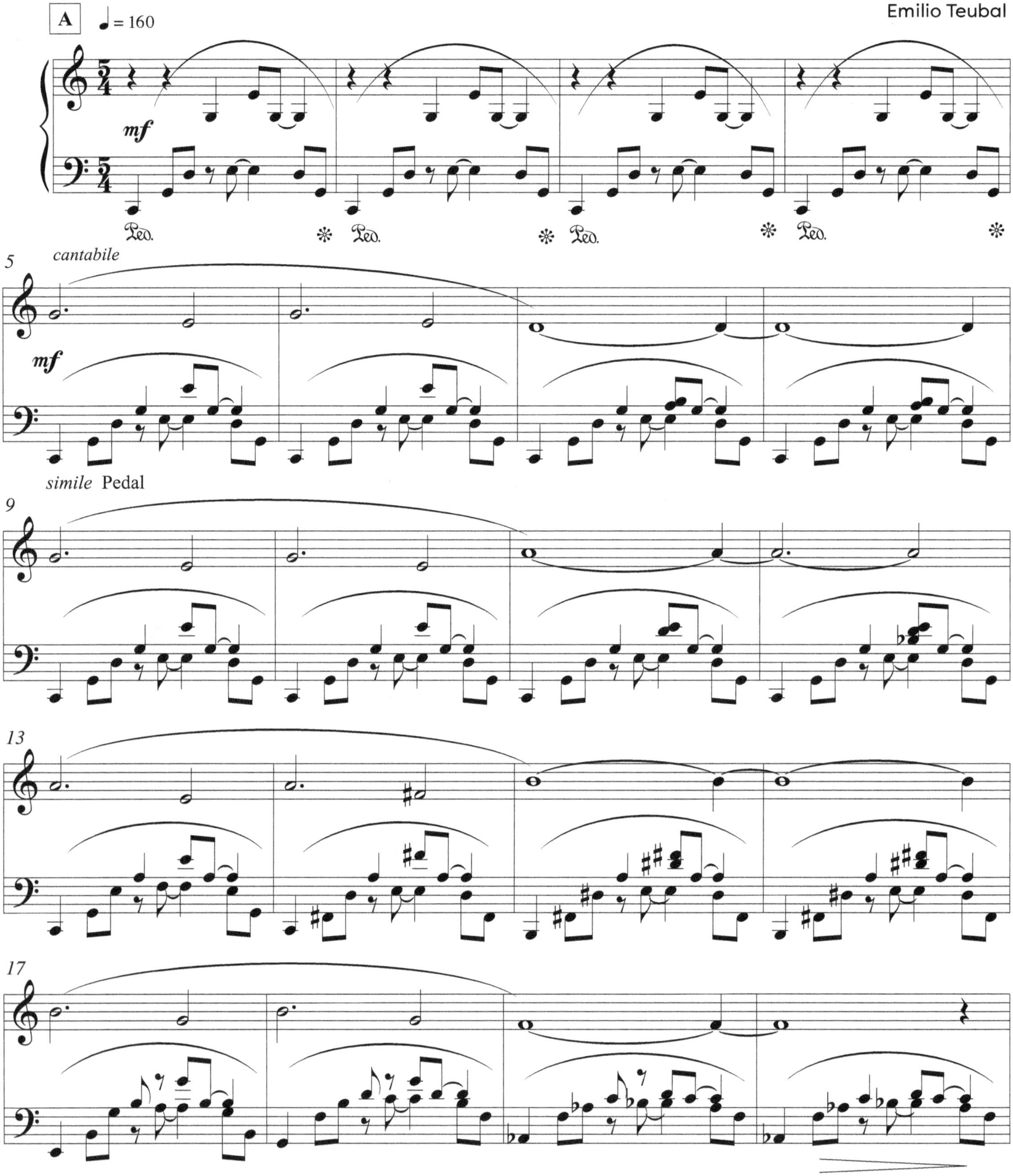

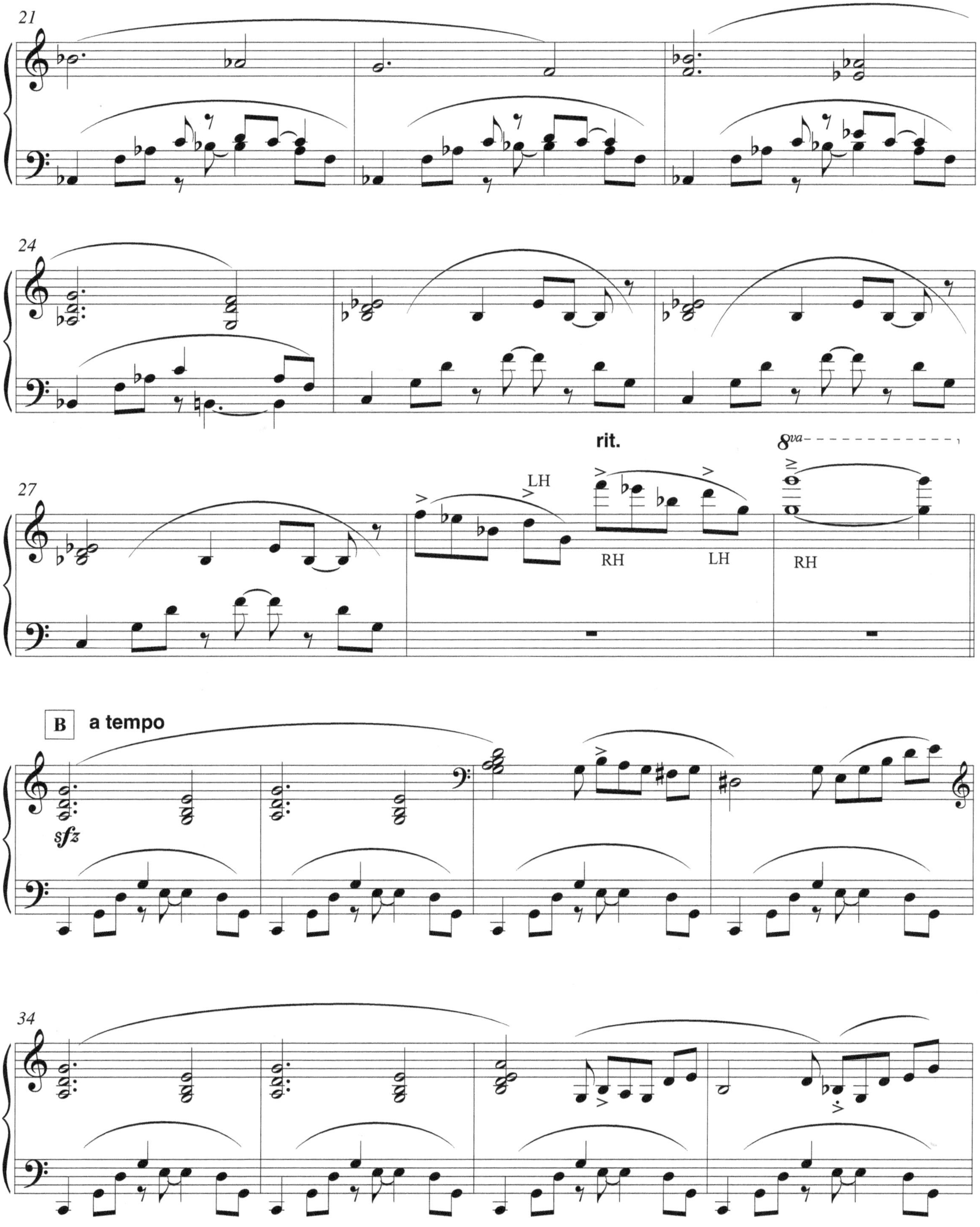
21
24
rit.
27
LH
RH
LH
8va
RH
B
a tempo
sfz
34

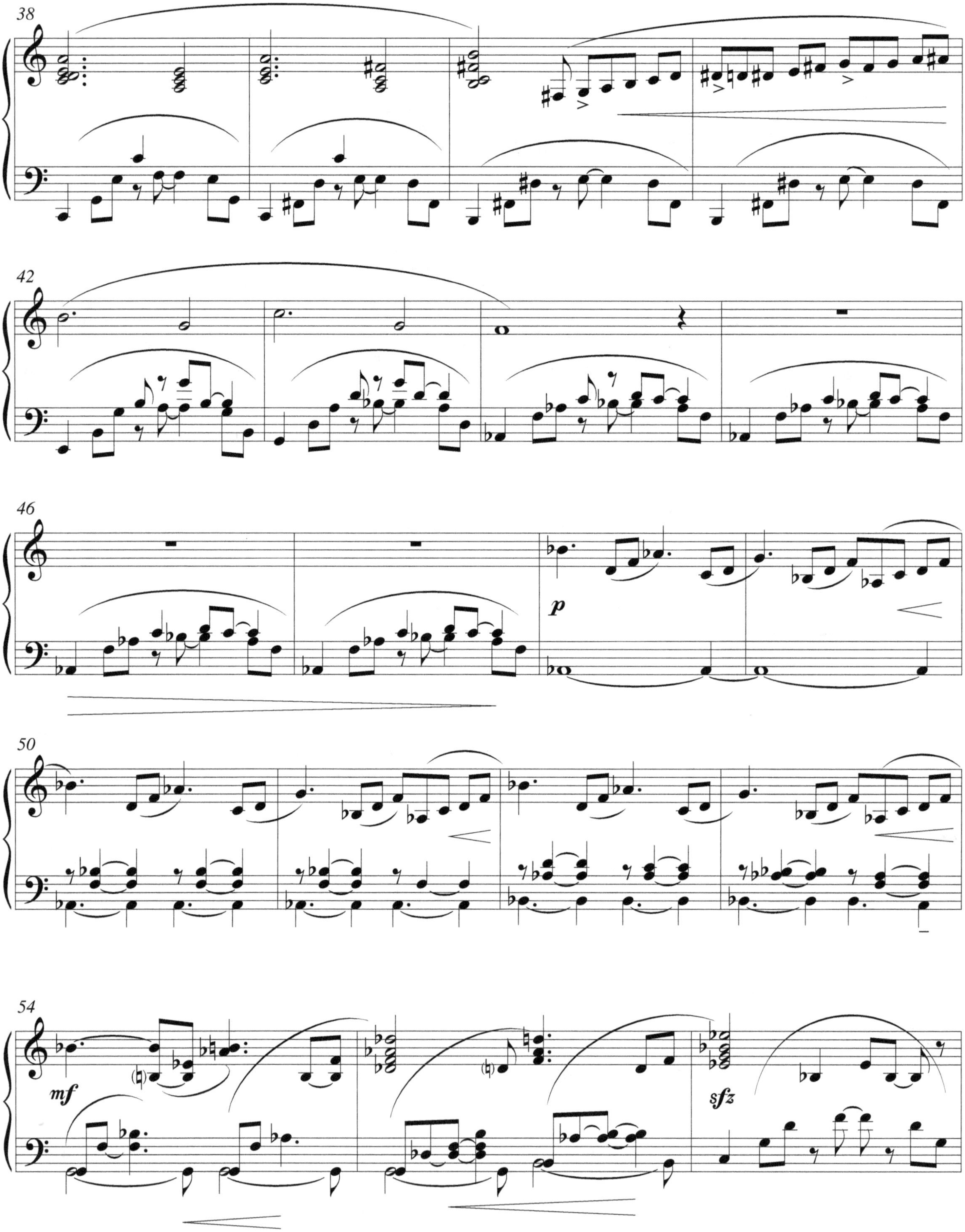
38
42
46
p
50
54
mf
sfz

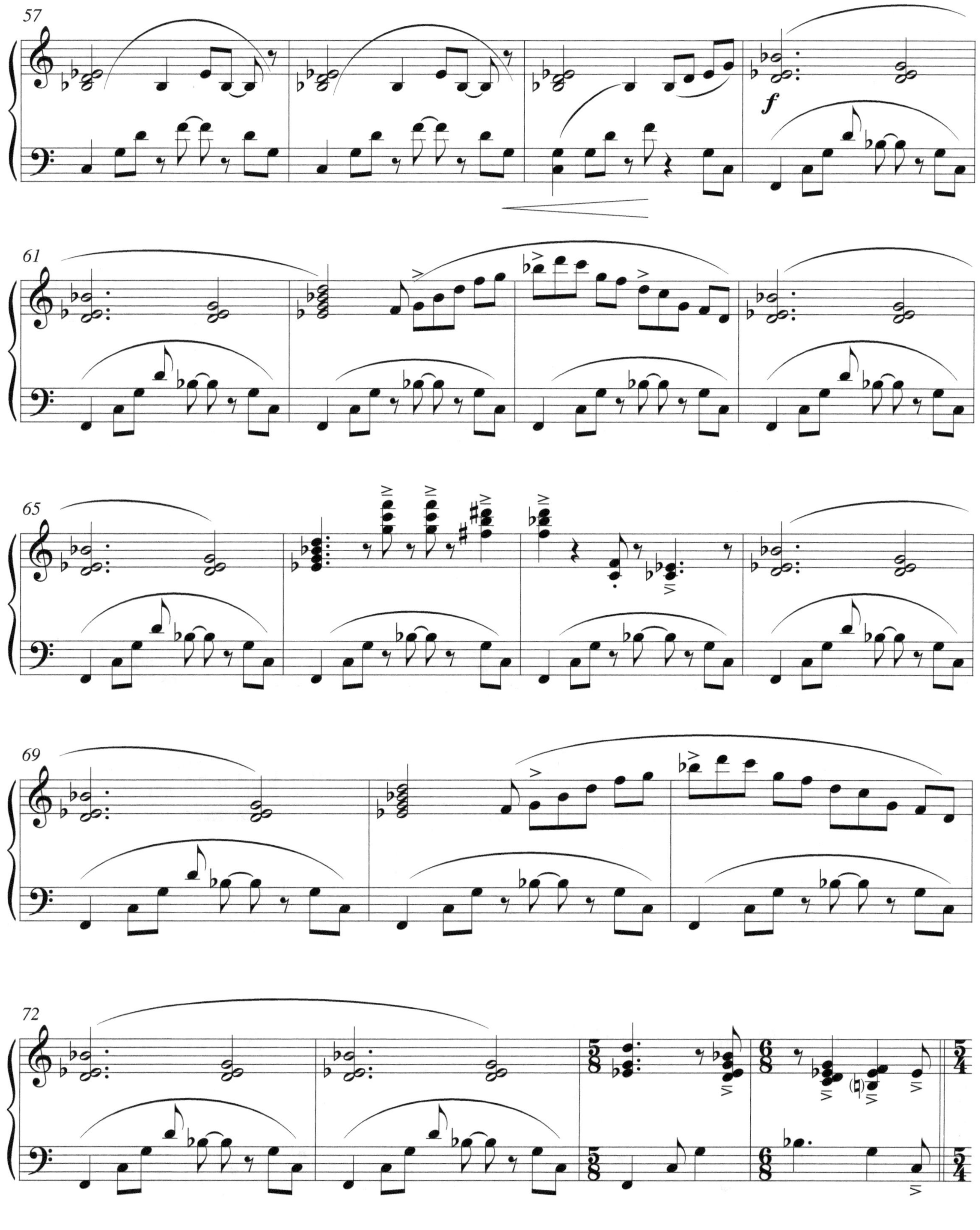
57
61
65
69
72

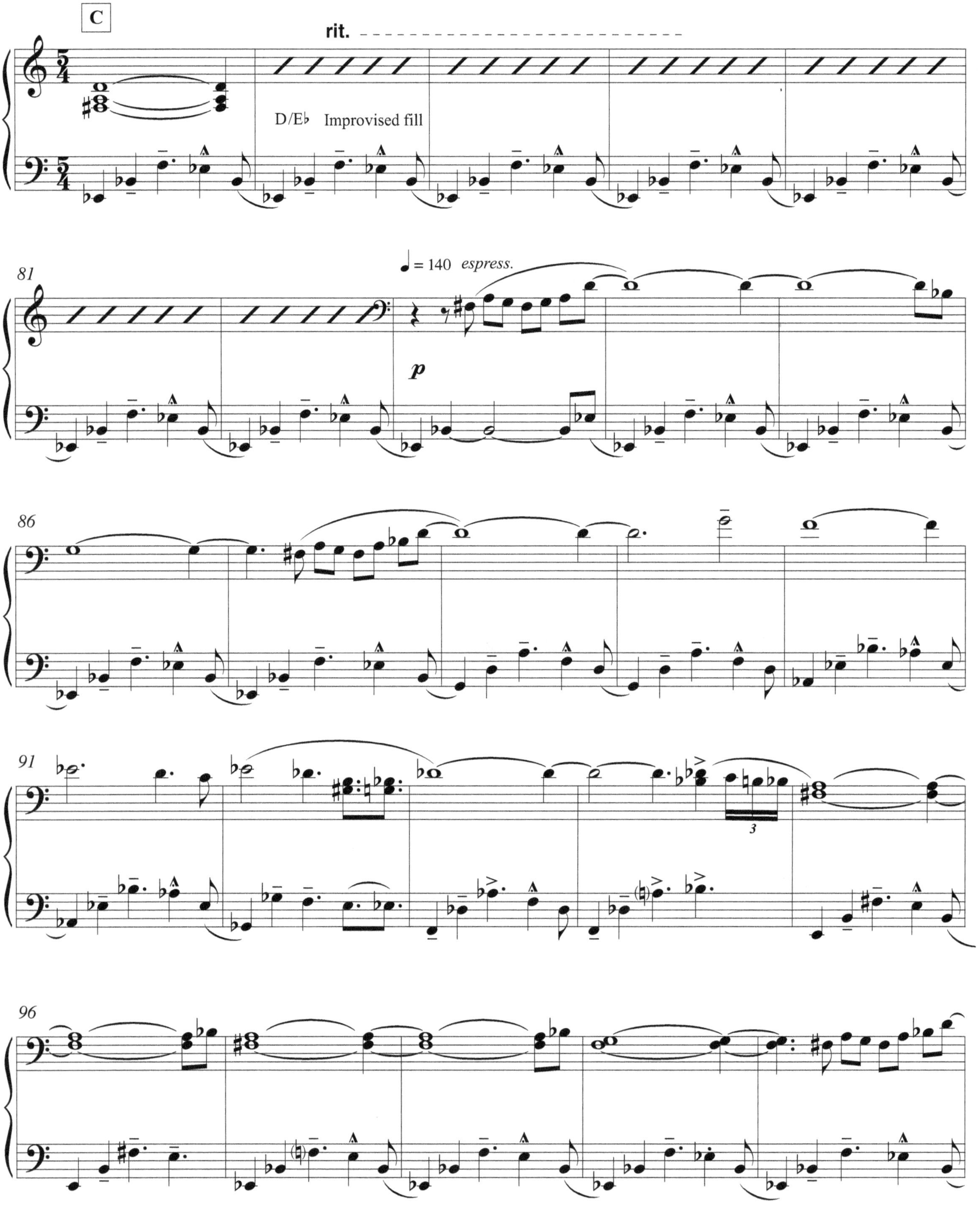
C
rit.
D/E♭ Improvised fill
81
♩= 140 espress.
p
86
91
3
96

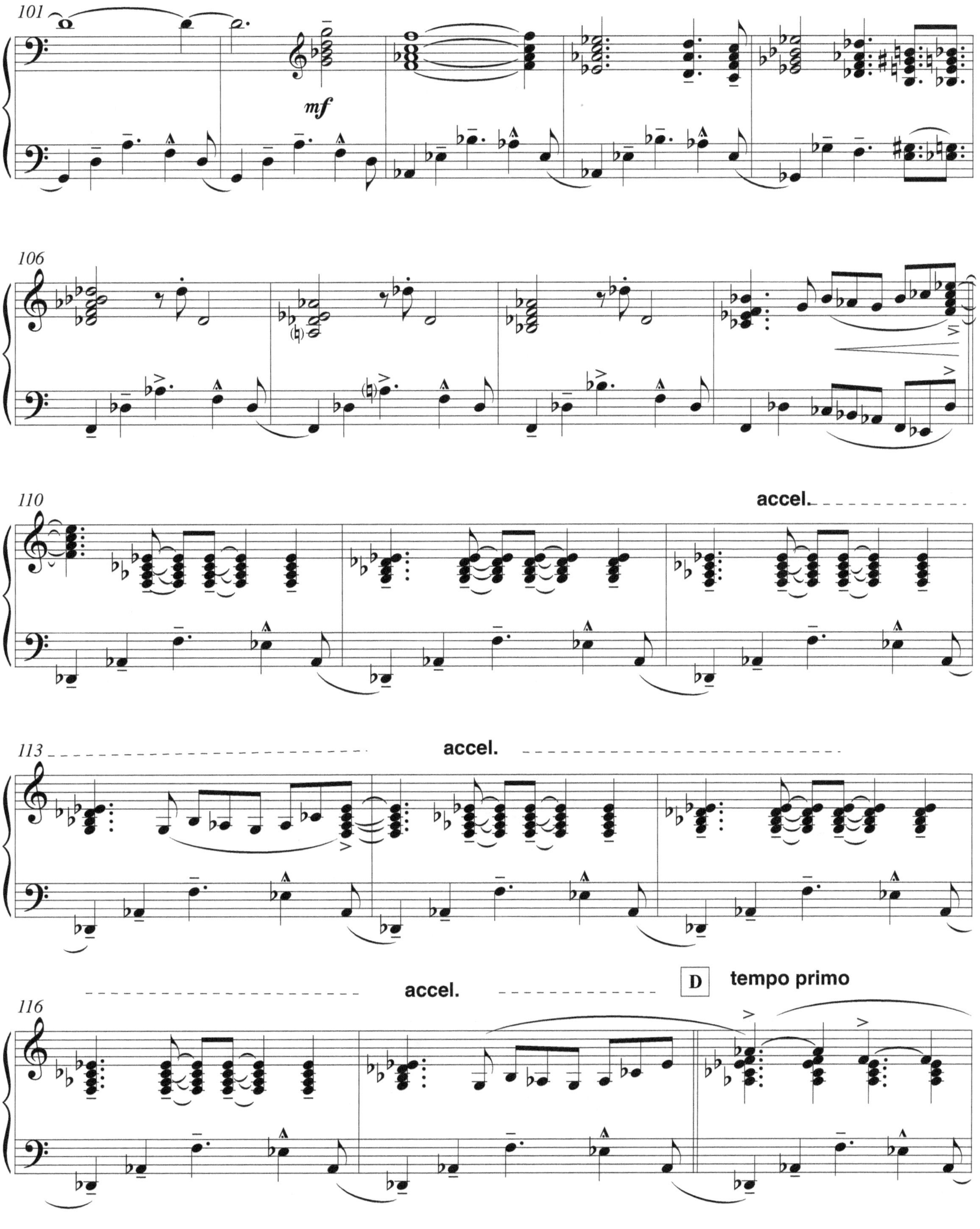
101
mf
106
110
accel.
113
accel.
116
accel.
D
tempo primo

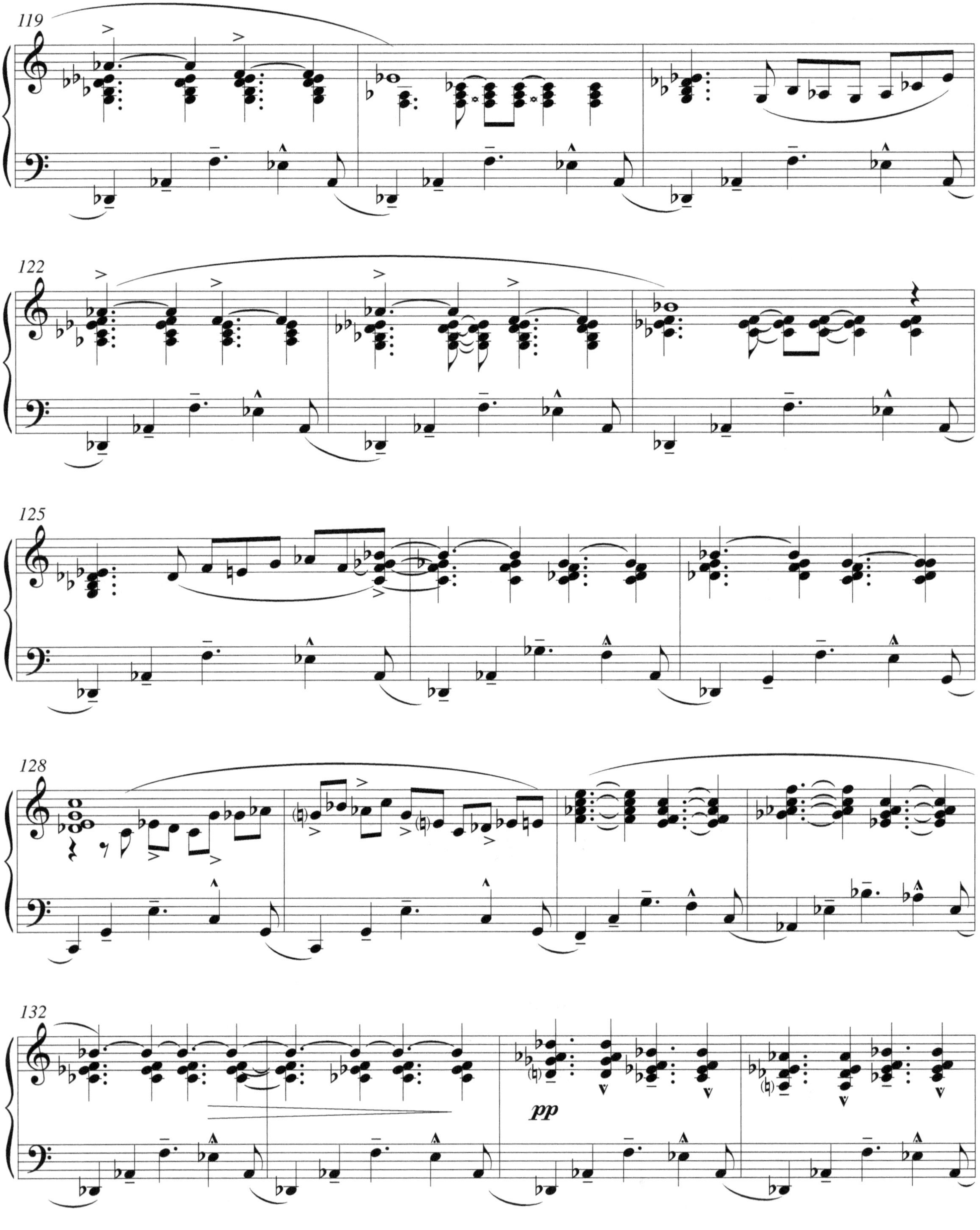
119
122
125
128
132
pp

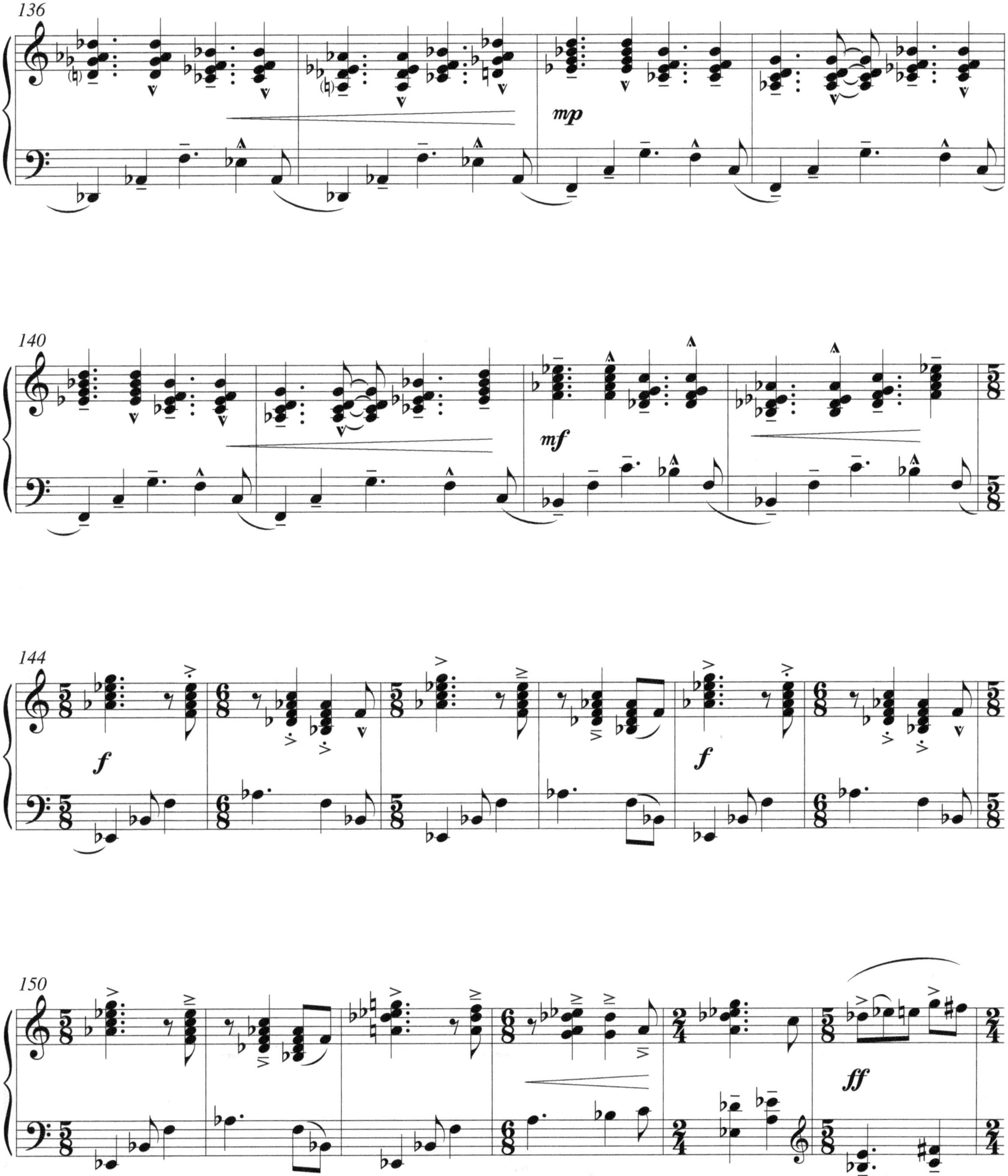
136
mp
140
mf
144
f
f
150
ff

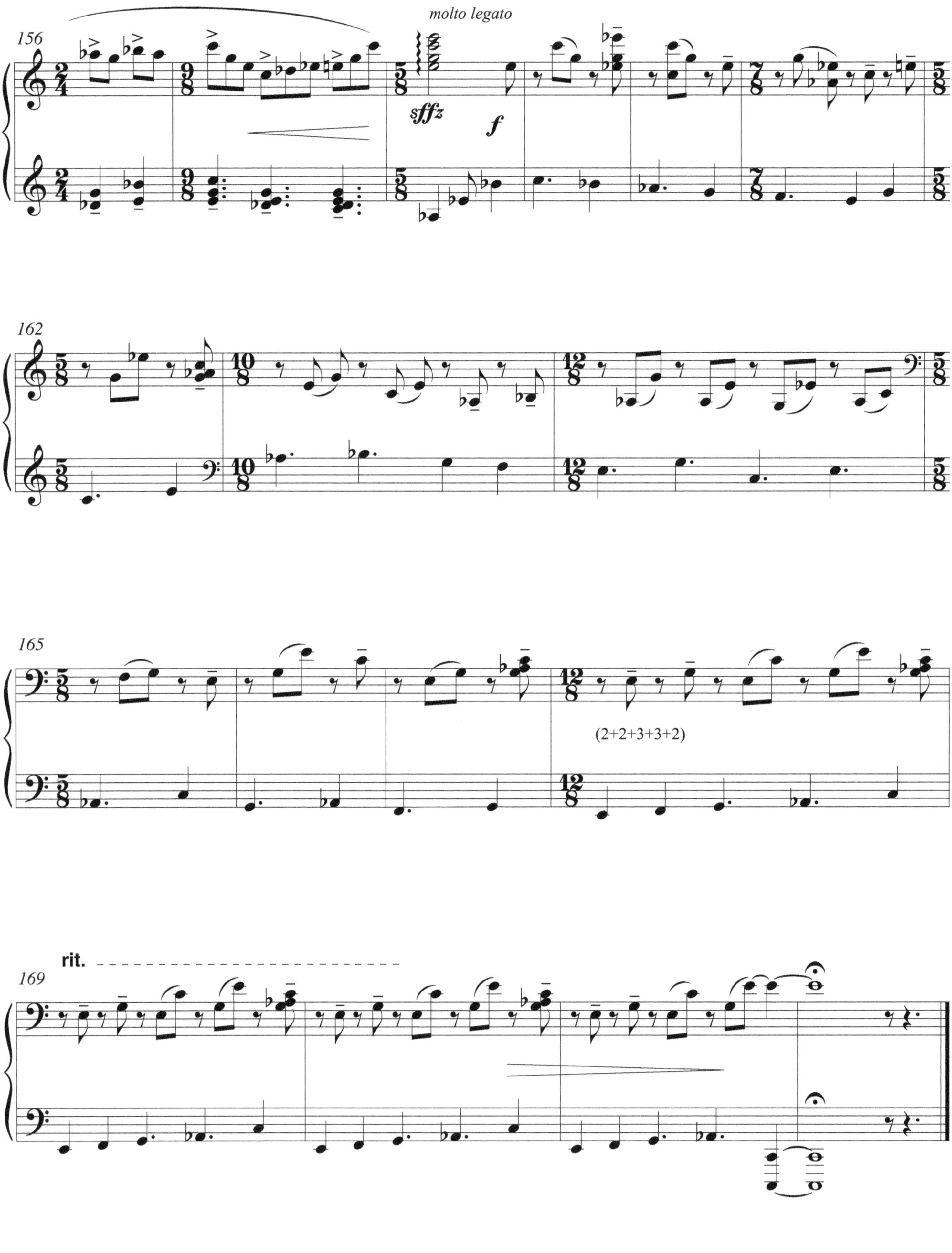
molto legato
156
sffz
f
162
165
(2+2+3+3+2)
rit.
169

THANKS

Cara and Alex Rearick, Felipe Traine,
Juliana Garber, Pablo Lapegna, Miguel Teubal,
Julian Teubal and Tupac Teubal for the title of "Rio."

www.ingramcontent.com/pod-product-compliance
Lightning Source LLC
Chambersburg PA
CBHW081341090426

42737CB00017B/3242